A Heart Returned

Memoir of a 9/11 Widow

JULIETTE BRISMAN
MA, LMFT

Foreword by Alice M. Greenwald
President & CEO, 9/11 Memorial & Museum

WIDOWED AND WELL PRESS

Copyright ©2022 Juliette Brisman, MA, LMFT
All rights reserved. No part of this book may be used or reproduced in any manner whatsoever without written permission except in the case of brief quotations embodied in critical articles or reviews.

Published by Widowed and Well Press

Produced by GMK Writing and Editing, Inc.
Managing Editor: Katie Benoit
Cover Design by Libby Kingsbury
Interior Design by Libby Kingsbury
Interior Layout by Libby Kingsbury
Copyedited by Cindi Pietrzyk
Proofread by Lissette Lorenz and Kelly Clody
Logo Design by Randi Burr

Printed by IngramSpark

Print ISBN: 979-8-9861737-7-1
Ebook EISN: 979-8-9861737-8-8

Visit the author at www.juliettebrisman.com
Write to the author at www.juliettebrisman@gmail.com

Author's Note: *This publication is presented solely for informational, educational, and entertainment purposes. The author has made every attempt to be accurate with regard to the events detailed herein and respectful to those lost in 9/11 and anyone impacted by the tragedy. Any errors, omissions, oversights, or mischaracterizations are purely unintentional. This work is from the author's memory and told solely through her point of view; other individuals may have different recollections and perspectives. The author has respected the privacy and preferences of parties who wish to be excluded from certain portions of the narrative. A few names have been changed as well.*

A woman is like a tea bag, you can't tell how strong she is until you put her in hot water.

—Eleanor Roosevelt

For Mark, who made dreams a reality.
And for our family, so we may remember.

ACKNOWLEDGMENTS

There are so many individuals who helped bring this project to fruition. For those who lent their support, encouragement, and guidance, I am truly grateful.

To Gary Krebs of GMK Writing and Editing, Inc.: Your professionalism and up-to-date knowledge of the publishing industry was a perfect match for my steep learning curve. For your role as an invaluable mentor, friend, and coach. For showing the care and interest in my book as though it was your very own.

To Katie Benoit, editor; Cindi Pietrzyk, copy editor; Libby Kingsbury, cover designer: For your diligence, attention to detail, and endless patience in working to get things just right, despite some unexpected challenges along the way. For the care in which you did so.

To Alesha Peluso and the Three Summers Creative Team: For helping me fine-tune my goals, challenging me to think in new and strategic ways, and providing insight and tools to help actualize these goals.

To Regina Madwed of Capitol Photo Interactive: For the beautiful professional headshots, as well as your patience with my seemingly endless requests.

To Randi Burr, artist: For your creative logo design, and also for being an important part of our lives.

To Alice Greenwald, President and CEO of the National September 11th Memorial and Museum: For providing the foreword for the book, the generosity with which you embraced the project, your thoughtful insights and your ability to put into words the spirit of the narrative so eloquently.

To Kenneth Feinberg, Administrator of the September 11th Victims Compensation Fund: For providing your personal endorsement, and for your incredible kindness and thoughtfulness.

To my incredible friends, both old and new: I can only attempt to express my heartfelt gratitude for your friendship. Coincidentally, during the creation of this book, I have, more than ever, needed to tap into the compassion, humor, and wisdom you have generously provided. I cherish each of you.

To my beloved family: I am profoundly impacted by your devotion, unconditional support and trust. It provides me the bravery to take on new challenges, step out of my comfort zone, and follow my heart. I love each of you.

To my precious children, Rachael and William and my newest son, Eli: For being living proof that significant challenges can lead to resilience and growth. For prioritizing me and each other in a way that has created the unbreakable bond we share. For always having my back and being both my biggest cheerleaders and fiercest protectors.

Lastly, I am grateful to the One that makes all things possible.

CONTENTS

Foreword by Alice M. Greenwald, xi
Prologue: Officer Henley, 1
Chapter One: Summer Rain, 7
Chapter Two: Sales Call, 17
Chapter Three: Mini Date, 27
Chapter Four: Balancing Act, 39
Chapter Five: Flying Rabbit, 49
Chapter Six: The Mystery Unfolds, 55
Chapter Seven: Separation Anxiety, 63
Chapter Eight: A Ring and a Reunion, 79
Chapter Nine: Wedding Bells, 87
Chapter Ten: Baby Brismans, 97
Chapter Eleven: Office in the Clouds, 113
Chapter Twelve: Missing Persons, 121
Chapter Thirteen: Picking up the Pieces, 135
Chapter Fourteen: Help Me, Rhonda!, 163
Epilogue: The Heart Returned, 177
Two More Gifts, 181
Postscript, 185
Photographs, 189
About the Author: Juliette Brisman, MA, LMFT, 201

FOREWORD

The day the world changed. That is how, in the immediate aftermath of the worst terrorist attack on American soil in this nation's history, people described the events and consequences of September 11, 2001. It is how, almost twenty-one years later, the day continues to be characterized. And it was how people around the world instinctively felt on that terrible day. There was an immediate, collective recognition that, going forward, history would be demarcated; there would now, forever, be a time "before 9/11" and "after 9/11."

But as far-reaching and universal the experience, for those most directly impacted by the events of 9/11—the families who had to confront the unthinkable loss of a spouse, a parent, a child—the world had indeed changed in ways profound and unalterable, intimate and painfully personal. Private grief would be experienced within the context of a very public tragedy.

Juliette Brisman has sought to reclaim the personal narrative of her experience as a 9/11 widow. She takes us with her on a journey of remembrance, recounting in vivid detail how she first met her husband Mark, fell in love with him, and began their lives together as a couple, as husband and wife, and as parents to two adorable children. The journey is not unfamiliar—dates at a mini golf course, the sadness of a divorce in the family, a first apartment, the ambitious pursuit of professional opportunity, the fear of not being able to conceive, and then the unbounded, anticipatory joy of expecting a first child. There is nothing particularly unique or exceptional in these moments, and perhaps that is the point. Juliette and Mark were living their lives; this was their story. Until it was not.

In every respect, 9/11 was an interruption of normalcy. On a brilliantly clear September morning, Mark had gone to his office on the eighty-fifth floor of the South Tower (Two World Center) in lower Manhattan. He would not make it home. But it is not the circumstances of his death that Juliette wants to share, it is how he lived his life. And this is the triumph of remembrance: We celebrate those we love with the stories we tell about them, and by telling those stories, we keep their spirits alive.

Mark's spirit is palpable throughout this memoir. He was a genuinely good guy, someone we would all have wanted to know. Clearly, he loved his family deeply, and that love, as we find out, transcends the boundary between life and death.

The day the world changed. In Jewish tradition, it is held that "anyone who destroys a life is considered by Scripture to have destroyed an entire world; and anyone who saves a life is as if he saved an entire world." With this poignant love story, Juliette Brisman has transformed the abstraction of mass death into something real and recognizable. She has, through her telling, saved a world of one.

—Alice M. Greenwald
President & CEO, 9/11 Memorial & Museum July 2022

Prologue

Officer Henley

Wall Street, New York City
1 Police Plaza
August 2004

It was a hot and sunny August day as I took Metro-North Railroad from Armonk, New York (technically North White Plains), to New York City's Grand Central Station. Accompanying me for the day trip was William, my four-year-old son. I had taken him out of preschool to join me because, frankly, I didn't want to head into the city by myself. I wouldn't say I was afraid, but rather, concerned about my state of mind and how I might react to the surroundings and reminders of the past. He couldn't possibly have realized at the time that I had brought him along for company, as emotional protection. I hadn't told anyone else where we were traveling that day.

I tried my best to spin the truth to William and hyped it up a bit. "We're going on an adventure!"

This did the trick. He couldn't have been more excited to have had a day outside preschool—a special excursion into the Big City with just his mom. It didn't occur to him that we were headed into the vicinity of where he had lost his father, Mark Brisman, nearly three years earlier, and I wasn't about to point that fact out to him. I made certain to button myself up and not give the slightest reminder of him or what had happened. I couldn't risk potentially making William sad or afraid of our destination.

We had great fun on the train. He opened his backpack and played with his Masters of the Universe and X-Men action figures for a while, quietly acting out scenes of the struggle between good and evil. Although I usually didn't give my kids an excess of sugary foods, I made an exception that day and handed him some fruit snacks and rollups to munch on during the trip.

William was very much like his father: self-reliant and emotionally balanced. No tantrums, no outbursts. He didn't seek attention, validation, or acceptance, except from a select few people. He was mature for a four-year-old, but I suppose at least part of that was because he had already gone through more life experience and trauma than any child should ever have to endure.

I didn't feel sorry for him or myself during the ride. I was traveling to the city to verify what I already believed to be certain—that they didn't have anything belonging to me, and I was going to return home empty-handed. Lately, I had been feeling more disconnected from Mark—perhaps just because of the passing of time—which was making me feel somewhat depressed. My mood was especially low, as for years I had made a deliberate attempt to "stay positive" whenever I felt myself slipping. I no longer seemed to have the strength to keep up this front anymore.

When we arrived at Grand Central Terminal about a half hour later, I was stunned by the number of armed police officers and soldiers in military fatigues stationed there. Although three years had passed since the 9/11 terrorist attack, New York City was still on high alert. I felt safe and freaked out at the same time. At first, I worried about how William might react to the heightened security. In typical four-year-old-boy fashion, however, the sight of all the protection and weaponry electrified him.

One of the military officers, noticing that a little boy had stopped dead in his tracks among the hurried commuters and tourists, gestured for us to approach him. He knelt down a bit to William and explained, "Don't worry. We're here to keep everyone safe. There's no need to be afraid."

William remained unfazed. I knew he was more fascinated than fearful and that the soldier had been projecting what he thought was running in the boy's head. "What kind of gun is that?" William asked the soldier, who was more than happy to answer.

I zoned out of their conversation, preoccupied while trying to figure out the right subway line. A few minutes later, the soldier grinned and tussled William's hair, signaling that their exchange had ended. I thanked him and led William toward the sign indicating the Downtown 6 train. We raced down the steps, as we heard the train approaching. We made it to the platform just as the doors were opening and boarded.

The doors closed and the train lurched forward. My heart raced as this suddenly started to become real. All kinds of thoughts filled my head.

What will I find at the police station? Will it be something that connects back to Mark? How am I going to react to whatever it is—will I break down and fall apart?

On the other hand, I don't want to be disappointed. I don't want to have false hope.

I steeled myself, attempting to adjust my expectations. I convinced myself of the worst-case scenario and looked at the upside: *If nothing of value is revealed, at least I'm having a fun jaunt in the city with my son.*

William and I stepped off the train at the Brooklyn Bridge—Chambers Street stop. It was only a few short blocks to 1 Police Plaza—the headquarters of the New York Police Department—which was hard to miss: a bland rectangular building shaped something like an inverted pyramid. Inside, it was like any old police station: official, sterile, and bureaucratic with bulletproof glass separating visitors from the reception desk. I announced myself to the bored officer seated on the other side of the glass. A few moments later, William and I were buzzed in.

We were led down the drab hallway into what I can only describe as a faux staged living room in a repurposed breakroom, complete with mismatched couches and tables, reproductions of bland paintings on the wall, and ratty industrial carpet. I noticed a box of tissues situated on the coffee table.

Oh, I get it. This is a special room for 9/11 families. They are trying to be thoughtful and make me more comfortable here, even though it's a police station in the city. They want the environment to seem friendly. I appreciate the effort—but who is their set decorator? I guess they have a pretty limited budget to work with.

As we waited for the officer to enter, I encouraged William to sit on the couch, open his backpack, and play with his toys. He didn't listen, paying close attention to the room; he tested out each chair and couch for comfort, seeming to have received a burst of energy from the sugary treats and having sat for so long on the train and subway. He may also have sensed that my nerves were heightened. I asked him a second time to sit on the couch when the door swung open. This time, he listened.

We watched a handsome, thirty-something, clean-shaven black man of average build enter the room with a metallic box—kind of like a bank safety deposit box—in one arm and a thick folder in the other. I was surprised he was dressed smart casual in collared shirt and slacks without the requisite jacket and tie, like the cops on TV. He had just the right demeanor—he wore a pleasant expression but was not overly assertive or too jovial. He had obviously been well-trained on how to interact with survivor families.

He extended his hand for me to shake. "I'm Officer Michael

Henley," he introduced himself. "We spoke on the phone. I'm the evidence and property control specialist at the NYPD."

"Yes," I acknowledged, shaking his hand.

He gestured for me to sit on the couch. He placed the folder and box on the table as he took a chair opposite me. My eyes remained glued on that box.

What is in there?

"This is William," I introduced. After the fact, I realized my tone probably sounded somewhat apologetic, as though I was embarrassed about having him tag along for such a serious exchange. The officer nodded, seeming to not want to draw attention to William.

"Did you find us easily?" the officer asked. It struck me that he was engaging in small talk to be polite and put me at ease. I sensed he wasn't about to risk saying anything that might inadvertently upset me.

"Yes, no problem," I answered. "It's great to finally meet you in person. I admire all the work you are doing."

He shook off the compliment. Either he'd heard it many times before or was simply being modest. Either way, he was all business with semi-prepared lines. I was okay with it, as his self-confident, professional manner had a positive effect on me; I preferred not to have any emotions stirred up.

"It's an honor to bring some kind of closure to heartbroken families," he said. "I hope I will be able to give something to your family as well."

I struggled not to let my guard down. I couldn't allow myself to get my hopes up and then be disappointed.

What is in that box? Open it already.

"All right, Mrs. Brisman," Officer Henley said. "Are you ready?"

"Sure," I replied, wondering if I was prepared for this. As if I hadn't been nervous enough before, now I was terrified at what might be in that box.

The officer put a key in the metallic box, turned the latch, and opened the cover. There was a pregnant pause before his hand reached inside. I heard some jingling as he fished around for an item.

I closed my eyes and held my breath.

This is it. This is really it...

Chapter One

Summer Rain

Spit Club
Levittown, New York
June 1986

I didn't know it at the time, but in many respects my life officially began one dreary, rainy Thursday in the summer of '86. I'd spent the early part of the day working at my summer job as a hostess for kids' birthday parties at McDonald's, which wasn't nearly as bad as it sounds. I served the food, played games with the kids, and kept the festivities moving along. Sometimes I received between $20 and $30 in tips per party from parents on top of my regular pay. I was an eighteen-year-old, recent high school graduate, and I knew there were far worse—and much lower paying—jobs. I didn't have anything to complain about.

All that day, I dreaded my upcoming evening plans with my friend, Donna. She had received a new Trans Am for graduation and was eager to take it out as much as possible. For me, it was a showery weeknight and the idea of doing what was then referred to as "the Turnpike" (basically driving up and down Hempstead Turnpike between East Meadow and Levittown to check out guys at stoplights and pop into an eighteen-or-over club) didn't particularly excite me. Besides, I had Rich—a newish boyfriend—at the time. We weren't a serious couple, but I didn't consider myself "on the market" either. I certainly wasn't on the lookout for a guy.

Donna was another story. She had her sights on a specific guy, Angelo—Ang, for short—whom she hoped to track down at the Spit club. She'd pegged me as her plus-one.

I arrived at my parents' house at the end of my workday feeling draggy. The pattering rain and light fog didn't help; I was in no mood to go out. I'd hoped Donna would ditch the whole thing, but I suspected that wasn't going to happen—especially when the phone rang. I knew it was her, even though we didn't have caller ID.

How can I get out of this?

"Hi Donna," I mustered.

"Hey, Jules, how soon can you be ready?"

She sounded ebullient, which wasn't making things any easier. "Well, it's been a long day and . . ."

"Let's head to Spit tonight," she cut in. "What do you think?"

"Um, you know," I struggled, "it's kind of nasty out there tonight . . . and Spit is going to be empty, anyway. Maybe we put it off and go some other time?"

"Don't be ridiculous . . ." Donna protested. "I've been looking forward to this all day. No, *all week*! C'mon, Jules, it'll be fun!"

"I know, Donna, it's just that . . ."

"Stop messing around—*you're going*! I'll pick you up in a half hour. See you soon. Bye!"

The phone went dead. Donna never did take *no* for an answer.

I guess I better start getting ready . . . nothing too elaborate. Why bother?

I reached for my go-to outfit—a white top to show off the tan, yellow miniskirt, and white pumps—poofed out my hair, added a dab of frosted pink lip gloss, and voilà, I was done!

Sure enough, Donna showed up at my house in East Meadow,

Long Island, thirty minutes later on the dot in her brown Trans Am. A graduation tassel hung from the rearview mirror. I ran out of my house with an umbrella over my head and hopped in the passenger seat. It took a couple of seconds to shake the water out of the umbrella before closing it up. No sense getting the interior of her new car wet.

She sped off while I was still strapping on my seat belt. I listened to the wipers squeaking away the light rain that fell against the windshield and the faint sound of Janet Jackson singing on the radio. I was about to reach over to raise the volume when Donna tapped the power off. She was in her usual mood to talk.

"What do you think of my outfit?" she asked. "Is my hair okay?"

"You look awesome," I flattered her. "I hope Ang is out tonight and we find him."

"I have a good feeling we will," she chimed in. "And maybe you'll find someone, too."

"Whatever!" I chuckled. "On a rainy weeknight like this? Not a chance. Besides, I have Rich."

"Oh, right," she considered. "You hardly ever talk about him. Is everything going okay?"

"Yeah, fine," I replied.

Throughout our conversation, Donna checked herself out in the mirror. She was a pint-sized brunette with an easy laugh and oversized confidence. While not traditionally beautiful, she dressed to the nines in the latest styles and was something of a flirt with huge brown eyes, thick applications of mascara, and ample hairspray. I tuned her out at as she babbled for the next fifteen minutes about Ang until we reached Hempstead Turnpike and turned into Spit's parking lot.

I took it as a bad sign that there were only about a half a dozen cars in the lot—probably including those owned by the club staff.

This place is dead.

Either Donna didn't notice the light turnout or didn't care. She turned off the engine and raced out of the car. I started to follow a few feet behind her, but she sent me back to ditch my umbrella. Not because it wasn't raining; she didn't think it would look cool for us to bring it and didn't want anything cramping her style. Seemingly, she didn't care that my hair wasn't as well protected against the downpour as hers.

We entered the club to the blasting sound of Pet Shop Boys' "West End Girls." The interior was what one might expect: darkened hallways, flashing lights, and dancing platforms of different heights. A bar was strategically placed in the center of the action.

Donna scanned the room expectantly, as if Angelo was going to pop out from behind one of the pillars. Despite the poor lighting, it would be impossible to miss someone, as hardly anyone was there. She tried not to seem disappointed as she murmured, "Well, it's kind of early."

Hoping to sound upbeat and supportive, I blurted, "Yup, maybe he'll show up."

"I'm going to check my hair. You'll be right here?"

"I'll get us some drinks and meet you by the bar," I offered.

"Drinks" naturally meant some form of soda. We were underage and couldn't get an ounce of alcohol in this place if our lives depended upon it. I headed to the bar and attempted to seem as cool and adult as possible while ordering Diet Cokes. The bartender had little else to do and filled up two glasses right away. Seated alone, I uncomfortably sipped the soda through a thin straw and waited for Donna to return.

My mind wandered to thoughts of the upcoming week. I hoped I could get home early enough to call my friend Jane and plan our next beach day. My blonde hair was in danger of fading, and I could use a refresh of hot sun to brighten it up.

Donna finally reappeared and we made small talk. The music

was so loud I couldn't hear her, so I just nodded along while sucking down my beverage.

My eyes wandered around the club until I caught sight of a pair of guys on the other side of the bar. They seemed around our ages—maybe a year or two older—and were hard to miss: Both were enormously tall and thin. They didn't strike me as the typical Long Island guys you'd find at a club like this. Both were clean cut and on the geeky side. The slightly shorter one wore a long-sleeved dress shirt with khakis.

I don't know why, but something compelled me to keep looking at them—maybe because the club was boring, and all of Donna's talk about Angelo was wearing on me. The guys also seemed to be having a great time by themselves with their sodas. Each one laughed heartily at the other's jokes. The more I looked at the shorter of the two, the more fixated I became. It wasn't an attraction, exactly; there was something alluring about his wide smile that caused me to zero in on him. I must have been staring a bit too long because he noticed.

He nodded at his friend, signaling with his drink that they should join us.

"Oh, shit," I remarked to Donna under my breath. "I made eye contact with one of those guys and they're both coming over."

"So?" Donna asked, slurping her soda and checking them out as they made their way toward us.

"I'm not interested in either of them," I commented.

"Eh," she shrugged. "They're kind of dweeby, but at least they're tall . . . and well-dressed. You like them tall, don't you?"

I tried to be evasive. "We could always get going, too, you know?"

"Ang may be a no-show," she admitted, placing her Diet Coke on the bar. She flipped her hair and added, "We might as well make the best of it."

The pair of young men were in front of us before I had a chance to protest further and attempt an escape. Not that it would have been possible since Donna didn't seem the least bit inclined to leave, and I was dependent on her for my ride home.

The guy I had been staring at jumped right in with a pickup line: "My friend and I have a bet—you and your friend aren't old enough to be in here."

I knew right away he was just kidding, as Spit was primarily known for being a hot spot for high school graduates and college undergraduates under the drinking age. I feigned being insulted and outraged. "How dare you—I'm twenty-two years old, can't you tell?"

"Sure you are," he chuckled, inching a bit closer to me. There was that wide smile again. I couldn't seem to get past it. "Is there rum in that Coke—or just ice?"

"Ice," I answered. "But it's Diet Coke."

"I stand corrected," he said.

After an obligatory half-pause, he introduced himself. "I'm Mark Brisman."

He seemed harmless enough that I could offer my real first name. "Juliette."

"I think I recognize you from somewhere," Mark said. "Were you at the John F. Kennedy prom—from Bellmore—a year ago?"

"Yes, I was—how do you remember that?" I asked, genuinely impressed that he knew who I was from an event that took place so long ago and at which we probably had little interaction.

"Well, to be honest, you were hard to miss because of who you were with—David. My friends and I were so surprised he got such a good-looking girl."

I didn't know whether to feel flattered or outraged. I never thought of David—my ex-boyfriend who predated Rich—as unattractive, although I was aware that others thought of him that way. "He's not bad looking," I protested.

"Are you kidding?" Donna chimed in, having overheard us. "With those big bulging eyes?"

"He looks like a toad!" Mark's friend joked.

The three of them crackled with laughter. Outnumbered as I was, I felt I had no choice except to laugh along with them, although I felt a bit guilty about it.

Shouldn't I defend my ex-boyfriend?

Mark leaned over in such a way to indicate that he preferred to speak with me one-on-one. We had an easy conversation and discovered we had several acquaintances in common—all from his neighborhood, the Merrick/Bellmore area. I was relieved he didn't speak ill about anyone other than David. He struck me as smart, self-assured, and mature. I thought of him as a guy who had his act together, but he didn't come across as cocky.

When the discussion about people we had in common dried up, we talked about our summer employment. He didn't have the usual snobbish reaction when I told him about my fast-food job. He kept right on smiling as he informed me that he was working at a jewelry exchange at an indoor flea market. He didn't seem to love or hate it but did enjoy sharing his future plans, which he laid out with a surprising amount of specificity: finish school at SUNY Albany, attend law school, pass the bar, join a firm, and become partner.

My future wasn't nearly as concrete; I felt so young. In a couple of months, I was heading off for my freshman year at Hofstra University. Other than hoping I would choose the right sorority and get along with my soon-to-be roommates, I had no idea where life was going to take me.

Our chat ended abruptly when Mark's friend elbowed him that it was time to go. Although his smile remained, I sensed genuine disappointment.

"Nice to meet you," I mumbled.

He seemed at a loss for words as Donna gestured to me that

she'd had it with this place and was also ready to leave. Obviously, Angelo was going to be a no-show and Mark's super tall friend wasn't exactly floating her boat. I followed her toward the exit when a girl recognized us and started up a quick conversation. We were about to resume our departure when someone tapped me from behind.

I turned around and looked up at Mark's expectant face. "Juliette—I was just wondering if I could have your number? Maybe I could call you sometime?"

I didn't think too much of it.

Why not?

I fished through my purse for a pen and a tiny scrap of paper. I leaned against a post and scribbled down my first and last name and phone number. He beamed with delight as he neatly folded up the paper and placed it snugly in his wallet, as if it were a twenty-dollar bill.

A couple of minutes later, I once again found myself in the passenger seat of the Trans Am. It was still bleak and dreary outside, which meant the wipers had to resume their work. As we drove out of the lot, Donna revealed her real reason for leaving. "Maybe we should try Malibu tonight?"

Malibu was a dance club near the water in Lido Beach, but I wasn't in the mood to dance.

"I'm really tired, Donna," I emphasized. "I'm sorry—I doubt you'll find Ang in any of the clubs tonight."

"I guess you're right," she sighed.

"What did you think of the guys we ran into?" I asked.

"Eh," Donna waved. "Should we do anything else? Go to a diner?"

"Nah, let's just call it a night."

"Yeah, fine," she agreed.

I felt relieved to be heading home. I was exhausted by that point and did have to work the next day. We had nothing more to say, so Donna turned on the radio. We eased back to the sounds of Eddie Money's "Take Me Home Tonight."

As the evening replayed in my head, I made a mental note to tell my Kennedy High School friends how funny it was that I happened to run into Mark Brisman at Spit. I thought about the scrap of paper I left with him and wondered whether he would call me or not. I didn't care one way or the other, but one thing lingered . . . I just couldn't seem to shake the memory of his expression.

What was it about that smile of his?

Chapter Two

Sales Call

My House
East Meadow, Long Island
June 1986

I don't know why, but I couldn't wait to report the news of my coincidental encounter at Spit to my friends—especially Jane. The two of us had been close friends since we met while working at Merrick Woods Day Camp in Merrick, Long Island, several years ago. She had an assignment as a paid counselor, whereas I could only describe my role as a summer slave. They assigned all kinds of menial random tasks to me, including helping in the morning with the kids, hanging up pool towels, sweeping floors, and cleaning bunks. Unfortunately, for whatever reason, they didn't think my services were worth any compensation. God knows what kind of life experience they believed I was receiving in return for my labor, but I didn't see the point of it and called it quits after only two weeks.

Meeting Jane had been the one upside of my stint at the camp. She introduced me to smoking cigarettes (fortunately, I didn't pick it up as a habit) and acquainted me with a whole new group of friends. I trusted her judgment about friends and guys. She was a down-to-earth girl and the first I'd met from John F. Kennedy High School. She regarded her classmates as competitive and status seeking, which is why she sought to branch out and find friends like me in other areas, such as East Meadow.

"Guess who I met at Spit yesterday—you'll never believe it," I began, breathlessly.

"Who?"

"Mark Brisman."

"Ew—Mark Brisman? Really?" she sneered. "He's so . . . nerdy."

I was taken aback. I didn't expect to receive such a dismissive, critical reaction. Not from her. "He's not so bad," I shot back.

Why am I acting so defensive about Mark? I barely even know him. Sure, I gave him my phone number, but I doubt he'll ever call me.

"Don't get me wrong, Jules," she backtracked. "He's not a bad guy, and I don't know him that well. He's just really into school and stuff. Believe me, I know the Kennedy people all too well. There's no reason for you to give him or anyone else from there another thought."

Wait. What is she suggesting? Does she believe I'm looking for a boyfriend? I was just thinking of Mark as a nice guy—a potential friend, I guess.

"Focus on Rich, Jules—he's cool," she continued. "And hot."

I didn't disagree with her on that front. However, Rich wasn't academically driven, even though he attended Nassau Community College. He had lots of disposable income assisting his father in the family carpentry business. He looked a bit like Sean Penn with shoulder-length blondish hair. Muscular and athletic, he was something of a bad boy who wore tight, undersized T-shirts and typically had a joint between his lips.

I let go of the topic of Mark Brisman, deciding there was no need to press further. Jane was right. I had Rich, and he was enough for the time being.

A week went by. Gradually, thoughts of Mark receded from my mind. That summer was a carefree time for me—and why not? I had just graduated from high school, the summer was upon us, and I had my entire life ahead of me.

The weather looked like it was going to clear up over the weekend, so my friends and I made plans to spend most of it at our regular spot at Point Lookout on Lido Beach. I expected we'd end up venturing out to Malibu at some point for a night of dancing.

When I told my dad, Martin (Marty) Steuer, about my plans, he gave me the usual speech in which he tried to convince me not to be the group's driver. We always seemed to have challenging negotiations about the car. Dad was something of a throwback to a more patriarchal time. He drove my mom everywhere—even to work, despite the fact that it was such a short distance she could have walked there. She didn't seem to mind, being somewhat old school herself.

His micromanagement of the car was odd because he didn't seem to care much about things other typical dads cared about, such as what boy I was dating. To a certain extent, I'm certain he was being overprotective because he was afraid I'd get into an accident. You'd think he would have grown accustomed to the fact that my friends and I were just typical teenagers who wanted our freedom. We never drank and didn't take drugs. Fortunately, Dad was unaware of Rich's pot smoking and, at least to my knowledge, my boyfriend was never red-eyed while behind the wheel.

"Why can't your friends take you dere?" he pressed, exposing his Bronx accent. Dad always said *dis* instead of *this*, *dat* instead of *that*, *dere* instead of *there*, and *dose* instead of *those*.

My father's accent may have seemed surprising to some people, since he otherwise used proper grammar in his speech and writing and worked in education. Originally, he had attended law school in the Deep South on a full scholarship. During his first semester, his father (my grandfather)—a cab driver—died of a heart attack at age fifty-four. While my grandmother grieved over her loss, she struggled raising my dad's two younger siblings and paying the bills, since my grandfather had been the primary breadwinner. Family members—including my grandmother—tried to convince my father to stay put and not give up his law school education. An uncle arranged a transfer to NYU Law at the low price of $700 tuition a year, but even that was too much of a financial strain. Instead, Dad moved back home and took a job as a history teacher to help make money for the family. Later, he went back for his master's degree and took a job working as an administrator for the New York Board of Education in the Bronx.

My dad was average height, around five foot eight or five nine, and thin in stature with dark hair and matching complexion. His accent and swarthy looks unintentionally made him come across as a tough, street-smart guy—possibly passing for Hispanic—which probably benefited him, as the students he encountered were primarily comprised of that demographic. Dad had a firm grasp of Spanish, speaking it interchangeably with English while at his office. Most often, he dressed professionally, wearing a shirt and tie. Since he worked in education, he would arrive home at around three thirty or four in the afternoon, even before my mom. he was always around to keep watch over my sister and me, especially in the summer.

"Come on, Dad, it's *fine*," I countered. "I'm a good driver. You have nothing to worry about."

Once he realized he'd lost the argument, he reminded me that I was forbidden to drive into New York City. *Ever*. I had already broken that rule more than once before—a fact he had been unaware of—but he had nothing to worry about this time, since we had no intention of heading to the city.

"Yes, Dad," I sighed. "We're not going to the city, just the beach."

He switched gears. "The car has no gas, it's empty."

"I just checked it—there's plenty in there," I insisted.

No matter how full the tank might have been, it was always empty to him. It could have had a half tank, but he would still say, "It's empty—there's no gas in the car." He was afraid I would run out of gas and get stranded. His mind always went to the worst-case scenario.

"It's not enough," he decried, handing me a twenty-dollar bill. "What if you get stranded somewhere without gas? Fill it up all the way."

I never considered myself spoiled or overindulged, but the car and my going out with friends were different matters. My dad paid for everything—car payments, repairs, oil changes, gas, etc. In the days before I had credit cards or use of an ATM machine, he never believed I carried enough money around with me.

"Other than the gas money I just gave you, how much do you have in your purse?" he asked.

"I don't know, maybe ten bucks."

"Not enough," he said, stuffing another twenty-dollar bill in my hand. "In case of emergency."

I didn't need the money, but I knew there was no arguing with him. I stuffed the money in my purse and sulked into the living room. Whereas most kids would have been thrilled with a generous father who handed out cash, the exchanges always left me feeling uncomfortable. It was as if my father didn't have enough faith in me to trust I'd take care of myself. I had to remind myself that he was operating out of fear and love.

I plunked myself down on the couch with a big sigh and commiserated with Jill, my younger sister by two years.

"Dad being a pain in the butt again?"

"Yup," I replied.

"Just tell him what he wants to hear and stop arguing with him—you won't win," she advised.

For the most part, Jill and I got along as well as any teenage sisters. I had long since moved past the fact that, while we were growing up, my mother had dressed us as twins, even though we weren't. Jill was tall for her age while I was short for mine, so we ended up wearing interchangeable clothing sizes. Otherwise, we couldn't have been more different. Jill was happy to hang out with her friends at each other's houses, but she loved school—especially science. As for me, I was an okay student but didn't care much for school, preferring social outings with my friends and focusing on my extracurricular theatrical activities.

Jill and I were about to continue our rant about our father when our one telephone—which hung on the kitchen wall—rang. Jill and I exchanged looks indicating that neither of us felt like getting up for it, since we weren't expecting any calls and were feeling lazy. We also heard our mother, June Fay Steuer (formerly Kornblum), puttering around the kitchen and figured she would get it.

My mother may have been the daughter of a self-centered Scarlett O'Hara–type Southern-born woman, but she wasn't like that, except that she was okay with family cultural patriarchy from generations back—which made her a good match for my dad. Mom didn't require anything too fancy. Practical and old-fashioned, she enjoyed caring for our family and being a devoted mother. She believed strongly in education, but also felt that ultimately a woman's role was to look good, complement her husband, and serve as a good role model for her children.

Interestingly, Mom had originally studied art at the Fashion Institute of Technology's (FIT) School of Art and Design in New York City, but she left that career to become a stay-at-home mom. Later, she took a job in the young adult section of the local library, where she handled clerical work and ran programs for tweens and teens. Although she had worked full-time since I entered middle school, she found time to ensure that we always had a clean house and home-cooked meals. During her lunch breaks from the library, she would usually go home to get a head start on preparing dinner for us.

She didn't entirely abandon art, however. Her creative nature came through in terms of her fine taste in home décor. She busied herself with home projects, such as hanging wallpaper, reupholstering furniture, and collecting knickknacks. Her main hobby was gardening; our small property became a showcase of lush and dense plantings that compared well to that of our neighbors. Occasionally, she would go back to her artistic roots, creating scenic backdrops for school plays and community functions.

Mom was striking-looking—a cross between soap opera actress Linda Dano (*One Life to Live*) and Snow White. She wore her dark hair shortly cropped and well layered. Her blue-gray eyes and pale complexion contrasted a great deal with my dad's. Mom was never without a full face of makeup and preferred brightly colored clothing with vibrant patterns. Flat, multicolored sneakers or shoes were her trademark. My family regularly teased her about her "clown shoes."

Mom ended up picking up the phone. Although I was too lazy to answer the call, I did have enough interest to eavesdrop on the conversation.

"With whom am I speaking?" Mom asked in a formal tone. Her follow-up sounds made me think it was a business call. "Mn-hmn ... yes ... mn-hmn ..."

Good, it's not for me.

Suddenly, she asked in a serious tone, "You know my daughter Juliette *from where*?"

I perked up.

"Mn-hmn ... mn-hmn ... mn-hmn."

I felt a compulsion to rise from the couch and head toward the kitchen as my mom awkwardly said in her sweet voice, "Oh, okay, dear. Hold on for one moment, please. I'll get her."

I entered the kitchen just as my mother was putting the phone down.

"Who is it?" I eagerly asked.

Catching sight of me, my mom picked up the phone and cupped the mouthpiece so the caller wouldn't hear us. "It's for you, Juliette. He has such a deep voice—he sounds like an older man. At first, I thought he was a salesman."

"Well, who is it?" I repeated.

"Some boy named Mark you met last week. He said he's from Kennedy High School?" she blinked.

My curiosity was piqued.

I wonder what he's calling about. Why'd he wait a week to dial my number? God . . . I'm so embarrassed my mother gave him such a hard time.

"Okay, let me speak to him."

She handed the phone to me, and I shooed her away. "Hi, Mark," I began. "I'm so sorry about that."

I recognized the voice right away from a week earlier. He *did* have a deep voice. He seemed to know exactly what I was referring to as he said, "Yeah, I should have hung up when I had a chance. Your mother is a tough one."

"Yeah, she is," I chuckled.

We laughed and engaged in random small talk: school, work, the beach. When that conversation began to fade, I said, "I told my friends I met you at Spit last week."

I omitted the fact that Jane regarded him as a dweeb.

"I'm sorry for not calling you sooner," he said, his voice going an octave lower. "There's been a lot going on over here."

I wondered what he meant by that but didn't dwell on it. Judging by his tone, whatever he was referring to was too private to discuss.

"It's fine, don't worry about it."

Somehow, he managed to change the subject to one of our earlier topics. We babbled back and forth for ten minutes or so until he blurted the question: "How about we go out sometime?"

Hold on. Is he asking me out as a friend or as a date? I really can't tell. Does it matter one way or the other?

My slight hesitation must have given him pause, so he reasserted himself: "Are you free this weekend?"

Yes, now it's clear: He's definitely asking me out on a date.

"My friend Neil and his girlfriend and I are going to Nunley's to play mini golf," he said. "How about you join us?"

All right, it's a double date. I can deal with that.

In that moment, it didn't occur to me that I might have been betraying Rich. Then again, we weren't exactly head over heels in love or seriously committed to each other. For all I knew, he was seeing other girls.

This was a simple decision for me. I didn't care what Jane thought about Mark. There was something about this guy that continued to interest me.

"Yeah, sure, I love mini golf," I accepted. "But you better be careful. I'm a really good player."

Mark seemed more than up for the challenge. "Well, we'll see about that!"

Chapter Three

Mini Date

Nunley's
Baldwin, Long Island
July 1986

I didn't regard my upcoming get-together with Mark as any kind of major romantic thing. In fact, I hardly thought about it at all in the days leading up to the event. I viewed the date as something of a one-time occurrence and didn't bother to tell anyone. We were playing mini golf with another couple and that was the extent of it.

Whatever relationship was forming between Mark and me during this time was so casual that it didn't prevent me from continuing to see Rich. He and I went to the movies and hung out together a few times with friends at the beach or in someone's house, where a summer party would inevitably pop up.

As Saturday evening approached and Mark confirmed our plans, I contrived a lame excuse to Rich about why I couldn't see him.

Since I worked on Saturdays, the arrangement was for Mark to pick me up at my house after dinner at seven. We'd meet the other couple at the mini golf course.

"I may be a few minutes late because I'm switching cars," he informed me earlier that day. "I want to take the banana car tonight."

Banana car?

My silence made it clear to him that he'd lost me.

"Sorry—that's what I call it. It's a 1977 yellow Datsun 280Z. It's not just yellow, it's *really* yellow," he laughed.

"Wow, I can't picture it."

"Just wait," he teased.

I arrived home from work, had dinner with my family, and prepared for a night of mini golf. Nothing too fancy, as it was a warm summer evening and mini golf is a casual activity. I put on a miniskirt and brightly colored tank top. For footwear, I opted for sandals over sneakers.

I ran down the steps a couple of minutes before seven to peek through the drapes out the side window. Since it was early summer, the sun still glimmered in my driveway. At first, I didn't see a car, so I started to walk away until I heard a motor approaching. On returning to the window, I spotted a car turning toward my house: a yellow Datsun.

It does remind me of a banana!

The engine turned off and a tall figure emerged from the banana. I was impressed by Mark's presentation—once again, well-groomed and wearing Chino shorts with a nice T-shirt, knee-high tube socks, and white Nike sneakers. He looked handsome with his hair parted neatly in the center.

I shifted away from the window to give him some time to make his way to the front door. I waited a couple of seconds after the doorbell rang to make my approach and open it. I didn't see any need for him to think I was overanxious and standing by waiting for him.

Mark entered the house with the same beaming expression he had that night at the club. My parents made their presence known for brief introductions and handshakes, but this time there was no third degree from my mother. Mark was a respectable Jewish college boy, so she didn't have any concerns. Their friendly exchanges were just a standard formality. Mark was cheerful and handled himself well, passing my parents' obligatory inspection.

"Gotta go, Mom! We have people waiting at Nunley's!" I exclaimed as we made our escape out the front door.

Ever the gentleman, Mark opened the passenger side door to allow me inside the tiny two-seater sports car. He closed it and then jogged around the front to make his way into the driver's seat. He could barely fit his elongated frame inside. His head touched the ceiling, and his knees were crunched forward. But he seemed unfazed by the discomfort as he turned on the ignition, shifted gears, and looked behind and side-to-side before pulling out of the driveway. I knew right away this guy had his act together and was a safe, calm driver.

I soaked in my surroundings. The car may have been old, but it was well maintained and immaculate, as if it had recently been detailed. Mark had the radio on low to 104.3 FM, the New York classic rock station.

A moment later I said, "You were right about this car—it's *really* bright yellow. It probably glows in the dark."

"Yeah," he snickered. "It's got a couple of hundred thousand miles on it—but the darn thing still runs pretty well."

"It's a small toy for such a tall guy," I remarked.

"I don't mind," he shrugged. "I'm the third person in my family to drive it. It's a hand-me-down from my dad to my older brother to me. I'm just glad I didn't have to pay anything for it."

We continued to make small talk. Our exchange seemed effortless, unpressured. It probably helped that he wasn't the usual nervous type of guy on a first date; his hands didn't seem sweaty and remained firm on the wheel. He spoke with unwavering confidence, although there was something circumspect and private about him as well.

It wasn't a far drive from my house to Nunley's, which meant Mark had to rush a bit to provide some background on the other couple we were about to see. "You're going to meet my good buddy, Neil. You'll like him."

"What about his girlfriend?" I asked.

"Oh, you mean *the wife*—Linda."

"Wife?"

"Sorry, I don't mean they're married," he explained. "She's okay, I guess. Neil refers to her as *the wife* because he can never seem to shake her. She's always there and around him."

"What's wrong with that?"

"Oh, nothing," Mark shrugged. "They dated for a few years in high school. Then he thought he would go to his first year of college and keep his options open—which didn't happen, because she followed him to school freshman year. Now he's back home for the summer and, *whadda you know*, there she is again. I hope you don't hold Neil's attitude about her against him . . . he's a guy, you know how it is."

I *did* get it. Women could be just as cagey in their relationships as guys. After all, I had been dating Rich who, like Linda, was more of a convenience than anything else. But I wasn't about to mention that.

"No worries—I won't judge him," I promised.

He turned his head to smile at me. I found myself returning a smile, breaking from my planned cool demeanor and, possibly, encouraging him. I shrugged it off as the car pulled off Sunrise Highway and into a parking lot adjoining the mini golf course.

Nunley's had a rich history dating back to the 1940s as an amusement park as well as a mini golf course. From our walk toward the ticket booth, we could hear Cyndi Lauper's "Girls Just Want to Have Fun" over the loudspeakers, kids screaming and laughing, some of the rides in motion, and a trace of the carousel, even though it was indoors. The main distinguishing image was the giant raised golf ball on a tee, which lit up with the word "golf" in neon letters.

Inside the gate, I noticed a couple pacing in front of the ticket office and assumed they had to be Neil and Linda. He had a distinctive elongated face, receding hairline, and saggy jowls. She was a brunette of average height and build who looked older than her years. She had a matronly quality that seemed to fit her "wife" nickname. Their proximity to each other indicated right away they were a couple, but their impatient body language and glazed expressions made it clear they weren't exactly lovebirds. Neil seemed relieved to see us, as if he was thankful he didn't have to spend any more time alone with his girlfriend.

Right after the boys exchanged high fives, Mark gestured to me and said, "Neil, this is Juliette. Juliette, meet my longtime buddy, Neil."

Neil perked up as we shook hands. I could tell he was sizing me up. When he was done, he shot Mark the typical guy expression indicating his approval, as if to say, "Not bad."

Mark, meanwhile, jerked his head toward Linda to signal that Neil better introduce her before he came across as rude. "Oh yeah," Neil realized. "This is Linda, my ball and chain."

Linda stepped forward, not minding the impolite reference. I assumed she thought it confirmed her expectation that someday Neil might marry her. Without even knowing these people, it was plain to see this was never going to happen.

"Nice to meet you, Linda," I cheerfully said.

"Juliette—I like that name," she reflected. "I think we know a lot of people in common."

We engaged in the traditional game of Jewish geography—which included a bit of high school gossip—until the guys grew bored. Neil gestured to Mark. "We should get tickets and stuff," he suggested.

"Right," Mark said, turning to me with a slight wink: "We'll be right back."

It soon became evident to me that the guys were talking about me, as Neil kept craning his head back to gawk and then reacted with emphatic gestures, including a thumbs-up. Mark playfully shoved his friend after each of his friend's remarks.

I felt a bit weirded out by the attention. When they were safely out of earshot, I asked Linda, "So . . . how long have you and Neil been together?"

"Oh, I don't know, a couple of years," she demurred. She tried to sound casual while changing the subject. "What are you doing over the summer?"

"I work at McDonald's—as a hostess for kids' birthday parties."

"Mn-hmn," she blurted, unimpressed.

Apparently, her job as a middle school tutor outranked my summer gig. *Whatever.*

Fortunately, this dull back-and-forth didn't continue for long. Mark and Neil returned, both flashing smiles and raising mini clubs and colored golf balls.

"Should we play teams? A couple team-up or men versus women?" Mark suggested.

"No," Neil countered. "It's every man and woman for him- or herself!"

"You better watch out," Mark leered to me. "Like I said over the phone, I'm going to beat you."

"I doubt that," I countered. "I'm really good—I've had some practice at this course."

"So have I," he grinned.

Although we were competing as individuals, we ventured toward the first hole of the course as couples with the men keeping score on pads with the nub pencils one would ordinarily find in a bowling alley. Neil and Linda played through first.

When it was our turn, I couldn't help but ask Mark the obvious question: "All right, what did you guys say about me?"

"What do you mean?" he smirked.

"You know *exactly* what I mean."

Mark looked me straight in the eye and answered, "Neil is very impressed. He said to me 'good job.'"

"I'm glad I meet with his approval," I said.

"Well, with Neil that isn't always so easy to come by."

I nodded, accepting my date's responses, and then taking my mini golfer's stance at the first hole.

As it happened, we fared quite well, probably because all four of us had played the intricate course before and knew all the tricks. The game was fun and competitive, especially when it turned dark, and the outdoor lights went on. We took the game seriously and were neck and neck, switching off who was in the lead throughout most of the obstacles—the clown head, the windmill, the kooky-kangaroo, and so on. Mark and I complimented each other on the great shots and didn't poke fun when we missed.

The guys tallied up the results when we were done and compared notes. "And the winner is . . ." Mark began, looking around at each of us individually with excitement. "Drum roll, please . . ."

Neil and Mark both made mock drum roll sounds and mimed holding sticks with their hands. "By only one point . . . Neil!"

Neil celebrated his victory with several fist pumps and pseudo fan cheers. Linda gave him a cursory hug, somewhat deflated by her loss and her date's showboating.

"Who was in *second* place?" I asked Mark. "It was only by one point—I'm happy as long as I beat you."

"All right, second place," Mark sighed, checking the scorecard one more time and raising his voice level: "Second place, by only one point, goes to . . ."

Once again, he and Neil went into their drum roll routine,

which caused Linda's eyes to roll. Both guys turned to me sharply as they called out, "Juliette!"

"Hooray!" Mark shouted, embracing me. "Congratulations, you beat me by three points. I finished third."

Linda's head lowered in recognition of the fact she'd finished dead last—though not by much. Mark had edged her out by just one point.

"Don't feel bad, Linda," Mark consoled her. "We were all on our game and played well. It was really close."

"Yeah, great job," Neil directed at both Linda and me. "Hey, look over there—a photo booth. How about we take a picture?"

"I'm in, if you are," Mark said to me.

"Sure," I agreed.

We raced ahead to the photo booth. The four of us squished past the curtain and into the cramped area. After we made physical adjustments and jostled our limbs to get into a semi-organized position with our faces in the camera, someone dropped a few coins into the slot. The flashes came at us in rapid fire, and we made the best silly faces we could through our ensuing laughter.

Mark and I exited, so Neil and Linda could take pictures together. Neil rose to follow us out but was drawn back in by Linda. Mark and I stood outside the curtain and listened to their laughter as the flashes went off.

When the pair emerged, Mark asked me, "How about we take a turn?"

"Sure," I said, not giving it second thought.

Mark and I slid back into the booth. This time, since we'd seen the mixed results of the other photos, we knew we had to shove our faces together to make it work. The flashes went off and we were done before we knew it. A few moments later, the machine cranked out the black-and-white photos. Mark and I leaned over each other to get a good look at them.

As we'd hoped, our faces were straight and center in the photographs. I was captured looking straight ahead with a pleasant expression—but not quite a smile. Mark was caught peering to the left, smiled widely, revealing his perfectly aligned, sparkling white teeth.

Hmn, not bad.

Since no one seemed interested in going on any of the rides, it was suggested we drive to an ice cream place. We rallied around the idea and hustled to the parking lot to find the guys' respective cars. We had no problem spotting Mark's, even in the darkness. We hopped in our respective rides and drove to Friendly's restaurant on Merrick Road in Bellmore.

The four of us squeezed into a booth and right away started kidding each other about the mini golf game. I felt a bit left out when the subject turned to college, since I was the outlier who had only just graduated from high school. My mood changed dramatically when the treats came out and we all dove in. I had my usual—a two-scoop butter crunch sundae with hot fudge and whipped cream—while Mark slurped down a large chocolate Fribble.

I don't recall what else we spoke about, but there was plenty of laughter as we enjoyed our frozen delights. When we were finished, the guys split the bill. Mark and I said goodnight to Neil and Linda, and then we started home.

Once in the banana and on the road, Mark shared more about his family. He and Michelle, his twin sister and debate partner in school, were really close; they were often referred to as "the M and M twins." They had an older sister, Jaci, who was out of college and working in New York, and an older brother, Steven, who had just begun his career in dentistry. Mark didn't discuss his parents, and changed the subject by shouting, "Hold on—this is my favorite song! Do you like The Eagles?"

"Of course," I replied. "Who doesn't?"

He took this as a cue to turn the radio volume up louder to The Eagles' song "Take It Easy."

A couple of seconds later, he began to freely sing along to the tune. I cringed. He was *terrible*. Completely tone deaf and off key. I burst out laughing at his uninhibited *a crapella*.

He abruptly stopped mid-vocal to ask, "Why are you laughing?"

"Well," I hedged. "I don't want to hurt your feelings or anything . . ."

"What do you mean? You don't like my singing? Come on, you can be honest—I promise, you won't hurt my feelings," he assured me.

"To be honest . . . no, you are not a good singer."

He seemed far more surprised than offended. "Really? I don't believe you. I was in chorus in high school."

"That chorus teacher should have been fired," I teased.

My criticism only seemed to encourage him to resume accompanying Glenn Frey. I admired that he was so comfortable in his skin and was willing to throw himself out there on a first date. While I didn't exactly melt, I did find it endearing.

The banana turned into the driveway and came to a full stop.

Uh oh, this is where it gets awkward. Is he going to make a move?

He shifted to face me and gushed, "I had a really good time tonight."

The words tumbled out of my mouth: "I did, too."

He seemed pleased enough to continue. "I'd really like to see you again."

"Sure."

"How about July 15 at Jones Beach. Do you have plans?"

I thought momentarily about Rich and our friends. I was positive we would end up doing *something* that day, but we didn't have anything specific planned out yet. "No, I'm available," I answered.

"Great—I'll call you and we'll set up a time for me to pick you up."

"Sounds good," I said.

He leaned over for a farewell peck on the cheek; I didn't consider it unwelcome. "Good night," I said, exiting the car.

"Good night," he repeated.

I felt his eyes locked on me as I headed up the walkway toward the front door. I paused and couldn't resist looking back at him in the banana car. He sat there with his wide smile, waving at me. I flicked my hand back at him and fumbled with my keys in my purse. As I resumed my walk toward the front door, it dawned on me . . . *maybe there's something here after all.*

Chapter Four

Balancing Act

Jones Beach
Long Island
Mid-July 1986

My summer schedule suddenly become hectic. Now I had *two* guys to juggle. I had hardly committed myself to Rich, as we hadn't been seeing each other all that long, yet I felt guilty about what was developing between Mark and me. I'd never been in such a predicament before; I never wanted it and certainly never asked for it. Still, there I was, being pulled in two totally different directions by opposites: one, a fun-seeking, superficial "hottie"; the other, a studious and thoughtful college boy. The last thing I wanted to do was hurt anyone's feelings or make a bad choice by getting too involved with either.

I'm eighteen, enjoying the summer, heading off to college soon . . . why do I need to pressure myself with this?

I made my decision: to not decide. Not yet. I didn't know which one to choose, anyway. I liked both of them. I decided I would play it out and see what happened.

When I told my friends about my date with Mark, I got little more than "Uh huh," which revealed their lack of enthusiasm. They didn't know or get him at all. I can't say I blame them; at the time, I wasn't sure of what was drawing me to him, either.

Naturally, my friends were interested in the overall dilemma of my dating two guys and may have secretly admired me for it. Unfortunately, no one seemed to have any words of wisdom I could use. I was on my own with this one.

During the week that followed my mini golf date with Mark, I alternated calls with both suitors, doing my best to pretend there was nothing out of the ordinary going on. I couldn't imagine what my mom—who, with her usual proximity to the kitchen, was nearest to the phone—thought about this. She never grilled me on the subject, dutifully shouting out, "Juliette, it's for you!" whenever the calls came in.

My exchange with Rich was not what I expected. He was struggling to figure out how to register for classes at Nassau Community College and organize his schedule. He assumed I could help him, since I was going to college in a few weeks.

Wow, I thought, I'm not a brain surgeon, but even I can figure out how to register for classes. He's probably too stoned to focus on it. I doubt Mark has any difficulty registering for his classes.

I tried not to be condescending as I walked Rich through the process. Once we successfully sorted it out, I said, "Why are you bothering with this—I thought you were working with your father and didn't want to go to college?"

"I don't—turnpike tech is probably going to be a waste of my time," he replied. "I'm only signing up because my parents want me to."

Back then, "turnpike tech" was a common reference to community college. Attending because his parents wanted him to was a logical enough explanation for us to change the subject. "Hey, you wanna go to the movies Friday night?"

"That'll be cool," I answered. "What's playing?

"*Karate Kid II* is just out," he answered with increased enthusiasm. "I'm pumped to see it. I loved the first one."

"Me too," I said. "Sure, I'll go."

"Great, pick you up at seven."

Not long after that conversation ended, my mom called me back to the phone to talk to Mark. I was thrilled to talk about something other than college registration—namely, the fun we had at Nunley's. Once again, he congratulated me on my win at mini golf. "But, of course, I do expect a rematch!" he remarked.

We made more small talk until he found enough of a lull to ask me out on a second date. "How about we go to the beach Saturday night?"

"Um," I paused. "Which beach?"

"Jones," he answered. "Pretty sure it's a festival night—music and a lot going on."

"Sure, I'll go."

Smooth, Juliette, smooth. Now I have two dates in a row with different guys. At least I didn't screw up and make them on the same night.

"Great! I'll pick you up after work."

I don't know how I thought I was going to pull this off. When Friday arrived, I simply did my best to tuck thoughts of Mark in the back of my mind, so I could focus on Rich.

I can do this. Guys see more than one girl at a time without a second thought, so why can't I see more than one boy at a time?

It was expected at my house, for every date of mine—no matter how long we had been going out—to come to the front door of my house, ring the bell, proceed inside, and receive the nod of approval from my parents. I guess they wanted to make sure my date hadn't morphed into a serial killer since the last time they saw him. When Rich made his way into my house for the check-in ritual, something unexpected happened—something terrible that I deeply regretted, even though it was well beyond my control. The shit hit the fan . . .

"Hi Juliette," Rich said, kissing me as he stepped through the foyer. "You ready?"

"Yep," I said, pleased that he didn't seem high—especially since he was going to be driving. "We just have to wait for the usual stamp of approval. Mom!"

"Coming!" my mother called back from the kitchen.

The moment she materialized in the foyer, I felt something was off. I just couldn't put my finger on it. "Hi, Mark, how are you?" she welcomed him. "Have a great time at the movies!"

Hold on one moment. Did she just refer to him as Mark?! Oh God, this is embarrassing. No, it's much worse than that. It's a total disaster.

I considered it a completely innocent, honest mistake. Anyone might have been confused with all the calls she received in a given day.

Knowing that it was unintentional didn't do anything to help improve my situation. I faced a serious dilemma. I prayed it had gone unnoticed—slipped right past Rich's ears—or that he had chalked it up to my mixed-up mother. I scanned his face for some sort of clue, but he remained stoic.

"We better go," Rich said, checking his watch. "We'll be late. I don't wanna miss anything."

"Sure, let's go," I agreed. "Bye, Mom!

We wordlessly marched out of the house to his silver Camaro. He turned on the engine and backed us out of the driveway with a slight tire screech, as was his habit. His tape deck turned on in the middle of Elton John's "Tiny Dancer"—one of his favorite songs. It occurred to me that I'd finally thought of something Rich and Mark had in common: They both loved classic rock. I thought it endearing that a tough guy like Rich would be so fixated on a sentimental song from Elton John, rather than something blaring and guitar-oriented from Led Zeppelin or Van Halen. He hummed along to the song as we drove toward the movie theater in Massapequa.

Maybe, just maybe, I'm off the hook . . .

No such luck. When the song ended, he shut off the cassette player and stared straight ahead.

No doubt about it: He knows. And he's pissed.

"Who is this Mark guy?" he questioned through gritted teeth.

I hoped he hadn't noticed that my face flushed, and my heart was pattering. I did my best to wave it off. "Oh, nobody," I dismissed. "My mom just forgot your name. She does that all the time. She's always mixing up names of people."

His grunt indicated he wasn't buying it. He seemed positive I was seeing someone else, which also meant he knew I was a liar.

I can't believe I just lied to his face. That was plain wrong. But what else could I have done? I don't know if I'm prepared to break up with him. I hardly know Mark at all.

Somehow, we made it to the theater without the conversation escalating. But I knew this issue wasn't done—not by a long shot. I assumed he was more anxious to get to the theater on time and enjoy the movie than in hashing this out with me.

I gave Rich a lot of credit: Although the tension between us was high throughout the evening, he sucked it up and bought tickets and popcorn for both of us. He might have been furious and mistrustful of me, but he wasn't ready to throw in the towel just yet. He also wasn't about to have his movie experience ruined by our looming situation. He thoroughly enjoyed the film and raved about it as we left the theater and made our way to the parking lot.

Once the car was in motion, however, he picked up right where he left off. "I know you were lying before about that guy—Mark," he snarled.

Oh God, I'm so ashamed. I can't continue like this.

"I'm so sorry, Rich," I said, touching his arm. "You're right. I shouldn't have lied to you."

He wriggled in his seat in discomfort as if he had a bad itch—but he didn't swat my hand away, either. Now he seemed hurt more than angry. After all my effort to protect his feelings, I'd managed to wound him anyway.

"I don't get how you could do that—see another guy," he said. "I thought we had something."

"I don't know," I said. "It's not like we ever specifically had a discussion that we weren't going to see other people."

"Okay, well now we are," he countered.

"I'm sorry, Rich..."

He pulled the car into my driveway before we came to any kind of resolution. "So... who is this—Mark?"

"We have a couple of mutual friends and so we've been kind of hanging out," I fumbled. "I only recently met him, too."

"You can't sit on the fence forever," he cautioned.

"I know," I said. "But look, it's the summer. I'm going to college in a few months. I thought we were just—you know, having fun. I don't think I'm ready to be serious about anyone right now."

I thought my statement was fair, honest, and satisfactory—at least for the time being. We sat in the car in awkward silence as he processed our conversation. It also seemed like the perfect time to call it a night. I ducked out of an obligatory make out session, saying, "Call me" as I climbed out of the car and headed toward my house. He drove off in a puff of smoke before my key entered the doorknob.

Soon enough, it was Mark's turn at bat, on Saturday, July 15. After what had happened the other night with Rich, I prepared myself to avoid any slip ups.

On the other hand, I felt I couldn't keep this information from Mark for long. Withholding things struck me as just as bad as lying and wasn't at all the person I wanted to be.

I was surprised to find myself excited to see the banana promptly pull into my driveway. A few moments later, Mark rang the bell and I met him at the door. He kissed me "hello," which I welcomed. He looked immaculate, as always, dressed roughly the same as the last time but in different clothes: nice short-sleeved shirt, shorts, knee-high tube socks, sneakers.

The parental formalities commenced in the foyer. I was able to exhale when my mother identified him by his right name.

We headed off to the Southern State Parkway toward Jones Beach. Twenty minutes later, we found ourselves enjoying hamburgers, fries, and milkshakes at a stand on the boardwalk. It was still light enough for us to do plenty of people watching as we sat at a bench table and admired the scene and ocean waves.

Then we strolled hand in hand on the boardwalk and talked. It couldn't have been a better night: warm, no humidity, light ocean breeze, lots of stars visible in the sky.

Mark was right; Jones Beach was a happening place with happy couples and groups of friends everywhere, drinking, laughing, partying. Music was in the air wherever we turned—live performers, boom boxes, and even some emanating from the theater not far from us. But it was never so loud that we couldn't hear each other.

Everything seemed natural and effortless with Mark, as if this was how it should be. We caught up on our jobs, college schedules, and dorm rooming situations before shifting to our career plans and dreams. Mark had it all mapped out. He sounded like a man double his age as he stated, "I'm going to finish college, attend law school, pass the bar, land a job with a good firm, get married, become a family man, and have a dog—maybe two."

"Two kids or two dogs?"

"Two of each!"

We laughed at this, even though we both knew he meant it.

This is a man with a plan.
"What about you?" he asked.
"Oh, I don't know," I considered. "I'm too young to be thinking about marriage, a house, two kids, and two dogs. I haven't even started college yet! When I graduate, I plan to focus on my acting career, mostly."

"That sounds amazing to me," he said.

We moved to a secluded spot near the boardwalk where he made his move and leaned in for a kiss. We made out for a while until we were interrupted by some people nearby and went back to walking up and down the boardwalk.

The interplay between us seemed so casual and comfortable that I let my guard down and allowed the words "I'm seeing another guy" to escape my lips. Maybe I could no longer contain my guilt. Or I didn't think it was fair that Rich knew about him, but not the other way around.

Mark's reaction was quite different from Rich's. He registered what I told him, but didn't seem to be hurt, insulted, or angry. As he processed the information and played it cool, I felt the need to explain further: "Look, it's not serious. It only started with him a couple of weeks before I met you. It's short-term. Believe it or not, I wasn't ever looking for a boyfriend—certainly not *two*."

Mark stopped abruptly, having collected his thoughts. He eyes pierced through me as he said, "I really like you, Juliette. I want us to be together. If we're going to continue, I don't want you to see anyone else."

Huh? What? Two dates and he doesn't want me to see other guys?
To say I was stunned would be a gross understatement.
What about Rich? Where does he fit in, if at all?
"Um . . . like I told you, I'm . . . seeing someone else right now."
"I want you to break up with him. Stop seeing him," he said in a steady tone.

Wow. That sounds pretty controlling. What happened to my being a strong, independent woman?

My head and heart jumbled. I couldn't think straight. I had no idea I was going to be cornered into such a commitment so soon—*with anyone*. But I knew he meant what he said. He had made up his mind about me and wasn't going to allow anyone to interfere with his plans. I felt his eyes focused on me, imploring his desired response.

What do I do? I'm not ready to lose him . . .

"Okay," I blurted under my breath.

At the time, I wasn't fully on board. I didn't have the intention of sticking to what I had said. I was being pressured and needed time to think things through. My response was simply a way to escape the conversation.

Mark interpreted my "okay" as a wholehearted thumbs-up to our now being a faithful, monogamous couple. He grinned from ear to ear, overjoyed with his success.

Am I really going to go through with breaking up with Rich? I don't have a clue.

Chapter Five

Flying Rabbit

Jane's House
Merrick, Long Island
Late July 1986

I was conflicted by how I had left things with Mark. I had agreed to an exclusive relationship with him out of discomfort with the conversation. Afterward, I wondered whether misleading him had been a good idea; I didn't intend to get his hopes up. On the other hand, I didn't appreciate being pressured on the spot like that.

I turned to my friend Jane to talk things through. Rather than heading to the beach on a hot, sunny day, we decided to maintain our tans in her backyard. The homes in Merrick were, for the most part, set on larger lots than those in East Meadow. Her spacious backyard featured an immaculate, fresh-cut lawn; it was completely fenced in and private, with no immediate neighbors who might overhear our conversation. I knew we would have privacy there.

We put on our two-piece bathing suits and reclined on strappy plastic lounge chairs to soak up the rays. Jane had brought out two cans of cold Tab soda. While she gooped herself with baby oil and held up a shiny metal reflector to her already freckled face, I went the opposite route and slathered on Hawaiian Tropic #4 lotion to give my skin at least some protection against the sun. As we got settled, it didn't take long for the conversation to turn to boys.

"Soooo," Jane said, leadingly. "How are things going with Mark and Rich? Have you made a choice yet?"

"Ummm ..."

"I'll take that as a no."

"How do I explain it?" I sighed. "Things are ramping up pretty well with Mark. But he told me straight out I should stop seeing anyone else and had to break up with Rich."

"How did he say it?" Jane inquired.

"Like a matter of fact. It didn't come across as bossy or anything like that."

"How did you react?"

"I kind of said, okay, even though I'm not ready for that kind of commitment yet," I sheepishly replied.

"Eh," Jane dismissed. "Don't worry about it. It's not your problem."

"Really?" I blinked.

"I don't think it was fair of him to pressure you and put you on the spot like that," she reflected. "Like I said, it's not your problem. You can do whatever you want. Don't let him make the decision for you."

"You're right," I decided. "I won't."

My House
East Meadow, Long Island
Late July 1986

Thanks to Jane's pep talk, I was able to get my bearings and put my feelings for both Mark and Rich in perspective. In my mind, at least, I remained uncommitted to both of them with my options open. I planned to give Rich a fighting chance. I managed to talk him off the ledge after our last conversation when he'd driven out of my driveway in a huff.

"I hardly even know Mark," I stressed to Rich on the phone. "We happen to be in contact with a lot of the same people, that's all. He and I are just friends."

All right, I admit it, that was a little white lie. Mark and I were a bit more than just friends. But I wasn't willing to give up on either one of them . . . not yet.

"Good," Rich responded, sounding relieved. "Hey, it's coming up on two months since we met. We should do something special to celebrate, I know a great place for dinner."

"Sure," I agreed, impressed that he was thinking about something as sentimental as our two-month anniversary. "Sounds like a plan—surprise me."

"Got it! Bye!" he said, hanging up.

Early that Friday morning, my mother found a strange object at the doorstep of our house. It took a couple of seconds for her to register what it was and figure out why it was there. She brought it inside and called upstairs, "Juliette! You have a present!"

"What?!" I shouted down the stairs. "Are you sure it's for me? What is it? Who is it from?"

"Why don't you come down and find out for yourself," she teased.

"I can't! I'm getting ready for work," I stated, brushing my hair in the mirror. "Can't you bring it up?"

"All right," she sighed.

As my mother clomped up the stairs, my mind raced to what it might be and who it might be from. I found out momentarily when my mother stood in my doorway holding up a four-foot stuffed Bugs Bunny doll. "What on earth is that?" I asked, even though I knew full well what it was.

"Bugs Bunny, I'm pretty sure," my mother said. "A gift for you from Rich on your . . . anniversary? I didn't even know the two of you have been together long enough for any kind of anniversary. I'm sorry, I had to read the card to know who it was for."

My mother approached me with the doll, placing it in my hands. The material felt cheap and thin, and I could tell it was filled with cheap pellets.

"I don't want this piece of crap," I spat.

"I think it's kind of cute," my mother contradicted.

"No, it's not cute!" I shouted, tossing the offensive toy on the ground.

"Juliette!" my mother gasped. "Aren't you going to read the card?"

"What difference does it make? This thing is awful."

She picked up Bugs and handed it to me so I could read the hastily scribbled card affixed to it: "Dear Juliette: Happy anniversary. Rich."

"What do you think?"

"This is what I think!" I shouted, racing to the hallway with the stuffed animal and flinging it down the stairs.

"Hey, watch it!" I heard my sister shout from the bottom of the landing.

"Sorry," I called back.

In retrospect, my reaction to the present may have been too harsh. Then again, I was only eighteen years old. I guess I expected more out of Rich. He was supposed to be upping his game with Mark in the picture, and here he was gifting me with what I considered to be junk. I suspected he didn't even buy it. Either he had it lying around his house or had won it somewhere. More than that, it didn't sit well with me because he couldn't have chosen a less desirable gift for me. I had zero interest in cartoons or Loony Tunes characters—never mentioning them once. It felt babyish, like I was a five-year-old kid and not his college-bound girlfriend. It was as if he didn't know me at all. I didn't expect or want anything fancy like expensive jewelry—I wasn't materialistic—but this seemed cheesy and insincere. Flowers of any variety would have been a better choice.

This is how he tries to get my attention and win me over?

The Rich versus Mark decision now seemed like a simple one. Rich had knocked himself out of the running. The more I thought about it, the more I realized that Mark would never in a million years have given me a stuffed rabbit. He seemed to know me much better than Rich—and had done so in a lesser amount of time.

The rabbit was the stuffed animal that broke the camel's back. Recognizing that we were a mismatch, I made up my mind to break up with Rich before our "anniversary" dinner and not prolong the inevitable. I didn't want to see him again.

Surprisingly, I didn't feel the least bit nervous as I went downstairs to the kitchen, picked up the wall phone, and dialed his number. A voice answered on the first ring: "Hello?"

"Rich?"

"Yeah. Juliette? What's up?"

"Rich," I jumped in, wanting to cut to the chase. "I have something to tell you."

"Okay," he responded.

"I don't think we should see each other anymore. I really don't feel you are as interested in me as I would like you to be."

"Uh-huh . . ."

I wondered whether I'd caught him off guard and shocked him into a stupor. He might have been terribly hurt. Or, quite possibly, he just didn't care enough to fight for me. I knew he was an unemotional guy—"too cool for school"—but I didn't expect an "uh-huh" or silence. You'd think he might have said *something* to save the relationship or at least defend himself. We'd shared several fun experiences together over the past couple of months. I'd even met his entire family and got along well with them.

But he gave me nothing. I had to fill the space with my voice.

"Are you listening to me? I said, I'm breaking up with you."

"Uh-huh..."

"I know it probably sounds silly, but the stuffed rabbit was all wrong for me. You bring that as a present for a little baby—not for your *girlfriend*...."

"Uh-huh..."

"I thought you probably found it in your attic or something. Or did you win it at a carnival? Either way, it just shows how little you know about me and how little you care."

"Uh-huh..."

Another awkward pause. I had nothing left to say except, "Well what do you think?"

At last, he said more than a hyphenated word: "You're going to do what you want, so what does it matter? What do you want me to say?"

"All right," I concluded. "I don't want you to say anything. Goodbye."

He hung up. Over and out—not with a bang or whimper, just a simple exchange of information. It took less than two minutes for me to be off the hook with a break-up message. I felt immense relief at the thought that I wouldn't have to juggle two guys anymore. It felt good that I hadn't parted with Rich because of Mark. I could simply enjoy my last days at home before college—and now I would have a real chance to get to know Mark and find out what was behind that wide smile.

Chapter Six

The Mystery Unfolds

Mark's Home
Merrick, Long Island
Early August 1986

Mark and I started spending more time together as the summer progressed, and I found myself seeking out his company. I enjoyed spending time with him—so much so that sometimes, before heading out for an evening of clubbing with my friends—which he didn't seem to mind—I would invite him to stop by my house for a brief visit.

Maybe I was fishing for the compliments that followed. "You've really outdone yourself, Juliette," he would say regarding my latest "club outfit," which might have included flashy costume jewelry or a brightly colored belt or scarf over a little black dress.

On one occasion, he arrived as I was using an iron to press one of my shoulder-padded jackets before heading out. He found this particularly amusing and snapped a photo of me with my camera.

"First and last time Juliette does domestic chores," he quipped.

When I asked him about his evening plans after seeing me on a weeknight, he typically responded that he was worn out from his job and just wanted to relax at home with his family. Before he departed, we would exchange some lighthearted banter regarding how I would keep the guys at bay, although he certainly didn't let on if he was genuinely worried about this. With one last kiss, he set off to his house in his banana car.

All along, I knew he was keeping a personal secret from me. He would say, "Things are really stressful for me—one of these days I'll tell you all about it." I sensed he was keeping his cards close until he believed we were far enough along in our relationship, and he was comfortable.

Meanwhile, I knew he was close with his twin sister, Michelle, and how they had competed as a team in the New York State debate championship while they were in high school, finishing toward the bottom after having been successful in their hometown. "At least I brought a bottle of champagne with me," he laughed.

Although they were twins, he was protective of her like a big brother. "We hung out a lot together in high school," Mark said to me. "I would tell her what I was up to with the guys, and she was always invited."

Gradually, Mark became emotionally available and began to open up more with me. I was surprised but excited when he invited me to dinner at his house in Merrick for the first time.

The Brisman house on Julian Lane was a traditional brick colonial on a wide-set, tree-lined street. It looked warm and inviting, even from the outside. The moment we entered through the front door we were caught off-guard by a middle-aged, balding man with blue eyes rushing down the staircase. Although he was not nearly as tall as Mark—maybe five foot nine and of solid, medium build—it was pretty evident to me this was his father, Jerry Brisman.

"Dad," he said in a friendly tone, "I'd like you to meet Juliette—my girlfriend."

The word girlfriend sounded nice coming out of his mouth. I

suspected it had taken some courage for him to have said it.

"Oh, hi," he said.

"Nice to meet you, Mr. Brisman," I responded, trying to meet his gaze.

"Likewise," he nodded, continuing past us out the door.

"Bye," Mark called after him.

"Let me introduce you to my mom, she's probably in the kitchen."

The house, with its high ceilings and rooms tucked out of view, contrasted with my own. At first glance, the brownish hues and other details reminded me of a 1960s- or '70s-era TV show set: brick fireplace, furniture that seemed relatively unused, and zero clutter or fussiness. We stepped into the kitchen, where the walls were covered with wallpaper accentuated with smatterings of black flowers. The light shone through wide windows leading to the backyard.

A petite woman in her early fifties dressed in a velour track suit stood by the sink with her back turned. Presumably, she was prepping dinner.

"Mom, I'd like you to meet Juliette. Juliette, this is my mom."

Roberta Brisman spun around, revealing her pretty face. She seemed to be a Debbie Reynolds lookalike with reddish-blonde hair and brown eyes.

"Nice to meet you, Mrs. Brisman."

"Nice to meet you, Juliette. . . . I'm going to grill tonight. What would you kids like? I've got hamburgers and hotdogs."

"I'll have one of each," I replied.

"Just a burger, Mom," Mark added.

How embarrassing—I'm going to eat more than him!

As I was discovering, Mark had an unusually small appetite for a guy his size. I wished I could have taken back my order, but it was too late now.

"Who else will be joining us for dinner?" Mark asked.

"It's just the three of us tonight," she answered. "Would you like something to drink?" he offered me.

"Sure," I said.

He headed to the refrigerator and peered inside. "Coke all right?"

"Sure," I repeated. I winced in my head, realizing I was repeating myself and needed to make a better impression on Mark's mother.

I have more personality than this. I guess I'm more nervous than I thought.

He poured Coke into two cups, one of which he handed to me. "How about we go outside on the patio?"

"Sure!"

I said it again! I hope this gets easier.

He led me through the sliding glass doors to the patio. Since it was still the summer, the sun was still blazing in the early evening hours, so it felt good to sit on a bench in the shade and enjoy a cold soda.

It didn't take long for Mrs. Brisman to pop out with trays of hamburgers and hotdogs and place them on the grill. She seemed to know what she was doing standing over the flame.

She went back inside the house, and we followed her. Mark began to set the table for dinner as I awkwardly stood nearby.

"Juliette, come help with the salad," Mrs. Brisman suggested.

I went to the sink, where I tore into the lettuce leaves and placed them in a bowl.

Mark engaged his mother in conversation. "Juliette is going to be a freshman at Hofstra this fall."

"Very nice," she said as she cut up other vegetables for the salad.

"She is performing in a student-run musical this summer too, Mom, and will be doing more shows at college."

"Is that your major?" she inquired.

"Yes," I replied. "Drama and communications."

Without looking up, Mrs. Brisman returned to the sink to check on my progress. She picked out a few brown leaves I'd missed. She was kind enough to mention it casually, but I'm certain she figured out that I'd never done this before. My mother had always shooed family members out of the kitchen, preferring to work alone, so I didn't know anything about food preparation.

As we waited for the final meal preparations to be completed, Mark came over and sat next to me at the kitchen table. I welcomed his hand on mine.

At last, dinner was on the table. We chatted as we ate. It became clear that mother and son were close; when she looked his way, her eyes lit up.

After dinner, we went down several steps into the family room. I told Mrs. Brisman that I liked where the room was situated and how cozy it felt, especially with so many beautiful family photographs of young Mark and his siblings displayed on the mantle. My praise caught her full attention. She leaned forward and began to fill me in on the house's history. It was built for them after they left their apartment in Brooklyn. She was proud to say that she had hosted many holiday dinners there with extended family. First and foremost, Mrs. Brisman was a homemaker and devoted mother, although she also mentioned that on occasion she had worked professionally as a bookkeeper.

Mark changed the conversation to our excitement about college. "The only problem is we're going to separate schools and we'll be pretty far apart, distance wise," Mark said.

This fact hadn't quite hit me until that moment. "That's true . . ."

"Don't worry . . . I'll drive back to visit during every break. I'll call whenever I can. And write letters, too."

I turned to him with curiosity. "Really?"

"You bet he will," Mrs. Brisman intervened with pride. "He's a good letter writer, you can take my word for it."

"Well, we'll see about that," I jokingly said, giving him a playful shove.

He laughed obligingly.

Michelle, Mark's twin sister, chose that moment to pop her head into the room. She and Mark were fraternal twins, but I could tell they had some features in common, including height; both parents were on the shorter side. One immediately noticeable distinction between the two of them was her billowing, shoulder-length brown curly hair. "Mom, I'm going out!" she crooned.

Mark lit up at the sight of his sister. "Hey, Michelle, I'd like you to meet Juliette—my girlfriend."

"Oh, hi," Michelle waved.

"Hi," I returned.

Michelle was gone by the time I turned my head for a second look at her. Mark seemed disappointed that she had other plans.

Mrs. Brisman excused herself, so I thanked her for dinner before she headed upstairs. Mark and I went down to the finished basement, where there was a big color TV.

Mark checked his watch before grabbing the remote. He lit up with excitement. "Fantastic. It's starting now," he said.

"What is?"

"*Star Trek*," he said, flicking on the TV and finding the channel.

"Oh," I sighed.

"You don't like *Star Trek*?" he asked in a nonjudgmental tone.

"I've never watched it," I admitted.

"Never watched it!" he shouted. "How could you have never seen a single episode?"

"Honestly, I don't watch much television," I replied.

"Okay, then, you're in for a real treat," he said, dropping on the couch. He patted the cushion for me to join him, which I did.

During the commercials, he rattled through some of the history of *Star Trek*, along with the characters, the actors, and other details of the show that had no meaning at all for me. I just smiled, rather enjoying watching him get so animated.

When the show ended, he lowered the volume on the television and turned to me with a serious expression. I braced myself for the worst. Something big was coming. Whatever it was had been weighing heavily on him, and he had been using the television show to relax himself, which he seemed to have accomplished.

"I feel so close to you, like I can really open up to you," he blurted.

For the first time, I felt he was lowering his guard and seemed a touch vulnerable. Usually, he was upbeat and confident—almost to a fault.

"I'd like you to," I said, leaning in and giving him my complete attention.

He cleared his throat and said, "I'm very stressed."

"I've been noticing something is up. What's happening?"

"I'll tell you—I promise. I'm just not ready yet. For now, all I can say is . . . it's really difficult for me. I'm under a lot of stress."

That was the second time he'd used the word "stress." I wished there was something I could have said or done at that moment to make him feel better. While I was dying of curiosity and worried about him, I knew it wouldn't have been right to press him under the circumstances.

"I will tell you this, Juliette," he said, shifting closer to me. "Having you with me has been helping me feel a lot better. The fact that you are in my life makes me very happy."

That was more than enough for me.

When he's ready, he's ready . . .

A few days later, while we were driving back from a fun day at the beach, Mark's upbeat demeanor suddenly changed. Oddly, he didn't put the radio on.

Something is going on . . .

He licked his lips and swallowed, as if struggling to figure out how to express what was on his mind. His breathing grew increasingly audible, which sounded strange amidst the sound of the wind through the sunroof.

"Everything all right?" I asked.

He inhaled and exhaled deeply to compose himself before saying, "You know . . . I've been wanting to tell you what's been on my mind for a long time. I just wasn't ready."

"It's okay," I comforted him.

After a slight pause, he declared: "I think I'm ready now."

This is it. Here it comes. I hope this isn't a shoe about to drop that will impact our relationship.

He spoke with great deliberation; every word mattered. His voice cracked as he progressed through the story. I listened intently.

"The week we met . . . out of nowhere, I learned that my parents are getting a divorce."

I remained silent, resting my hand on his shoulder, which had been so burdened by this turn of events since the moment I first met him.

It all made sense now.

I need to say something, offer empathy . . . but what? I don't have any advice or wise words to offer.

I said whatever came into my head, praying it would be enough. "I'm so sorry, Mark. No wonder you've been waiting to tell me—but I'm glad you finally did."

He seemed relieved to have finally gotten this news off his

chest. He began to ruminate more to himself than to me. I just listened as he poured his heart out.

"It's going to be okay," I gently reassured him.

"One thing is for sure," he said, his smile finally returning. "I'm so glad I have you, Juliette. I don't know what I would have done without you."

I felt special for being trusted with his innermost thoughts and feelings. I hadn't expected to be with someone who needed me so much at this early stage in my life. I was hopeful I could provide the support he needed, even though I didn't know how. At the same time, I felt closer to him than anyone else in my life. We had taken our relationship to an entirely new level.

Chapter Seven

Separation Anxiety

Mark's Home
Merrick, Long Island
End of August 1986

Our last couple of weeks together that summer were blissfully fun, although everything blurred together. We went on the usual dates—the beach, a movie, the mall, a couple of dinners out—and hung out in his basement, where we continued to become intimate. I learned so much about him during this time, including his fascination with gadgets and electronics—he already had a desktop computer, which impressed me—and had a fondness for expensive watches.

Despite what Mark had shared with me, he remained calm, cool, and in control at all times. I was living day-to-day while also imagining what my freshman year in college was going to be like. I was looking forward to it, except that my proximity to Hofstra meant I was on a waiting list for on-campus housing, which I really wanted. I didn't pay much attention to or count down the looming days until Mark would be heading upstate to the University at Albany.

The night before he was scheduled to drive off, I stayed over at my friend Jane's house in Merrick so I wouldn't have to rush to Mark's house to see him off. By the time I arrived at his house the next afternoon, the banana car was already more than half-filled with his stuff.

Mark—his characteristic smile widening on seeing me—burst out of his house with a duffel in one hand and a bag of fraternity paraphernalia in the other. (The dead giveaway was the frat pendants flopping out of the bag.) He emptied his hands at my feet to hug and kiss me, the exact moment his mother stepped out of the house. She granted us our moment.

As soon as Mark released me, Mrs. Brisman asked him, "Do you have your contact lens rewetting drops? I know how dry and irritated your eyes get."

"Yes, Mom," he answered with a roll of the eyes.

He went about his business loading up the car while his mother served as something of a foreman on the project, coming up with miscellaneous reminders about items he shouldn't forget. Although he was doing the heavy lifting, she was determined to participate in the undertaking and be helpful.

Soap: "Yes, Mom."

Shampoo: "Yeah, Mom."

Spare glasses: "Of course, Mom."

I felt for Mark as he went back-and-forth from the house with each new bag of items. I could tell he was happy I was there, but a sort of sadness hung in the air.

I also recognized my role in the proceedings as a passive observer. I stood by and watched as Mark sweated out stuffing his possessions into the open trunk and through the back-seat door. Whereas his mother had a clear-cut role, I presumed mine was simply to be present and supportive. It didn't occur to me to offer any help, especially since it was apparent he didn't need or want any. Not that I could have contributed much anyway, since at that time

I hadn't yet packed anything for anyone, including myself. Mark may not have needed his mother's assistance, either, but there was no chance he was going to deny her that privilege.

It didn't take long for Mark to complete the task. He was extremely pragmatic and organized, and didn't go overboard packing or overthinking anything. He closed the back-seat door, slammed the trunk, and announced, "Well, that's it—I'm all set."

His mother rushed over for a tight hug giving her son all the usual warnings: "Drive safe," "Be careful," and "Call me as soon as you get there" before returning to the house, leaving Mark and me alone.

Next was my turn. I broke down in tears as soon as he reached me with his beaming smile and gave me a warm hug. My reaction took us both by surprise. Who knew? This was completely uncharacteristic of me. It was the first time I ever cried for a guy, and I hadn't seen it coming. I'd known him for a such a brief amount of time—how had I become so attached?

He's going to be so far away. How will I deal with not having him close by?

The tears flowed. He held me tighter, holding my head into his chest and stroking my hair. "Don't cry," he comforted me. "We'll call each other.... I'll write as much as I can."

Although he was sincere in his empathy, I could tell that my reaction also made him feel good. It signified that he meant something to me. He was *special*. There was no doubt in my mind from that moment forward that both of those things were true.

We kissed and he gave me another squeeze before sighing, "I guess I better hit the road."

"Yeah," I sniffled.

My eyes welled up even more as he headed to the car. Not knowing what else to say, I repeated his mother's advisements: "Drive, safe," "Be careful," and "Call me as soon as you get there."

He entered the car, closed the door, and turned on the engine. Classic rock music blasted through the window. We waved to each other as he pulled out of the driveway. My eyes followed the car as it disappeared down the block.

I felt empty and alone. I totally lost it; my cheeks became drenched with tears. I sobbed as I plodded toward my car. I was so overcome I didn't go into the house to say goodbye to Mrs. Brisman.

I cried all the way home. I couldn't stop thinking about what a long drive it was for him to go to Albany all by himself—something like 170 miles. It would take around three hours for him to get there—without any breaks. I'd certainly never driven that far by myself and hadn't even spent that much time on highways. Albany seemed like the end of the world.

Along with being concerned for his safety, I couldn't shake one thought: *What am I going to do without him?*

Hofstra University
Hempstead, Long Island
September 1986–Spring 1989

Mark dutifully called me five or so hours later to confirm he had arrived safe and sound. We made some chitchat about his uneventful ride upstate before the conversation dried up and he said, "I can still picture you standing there teary-eyed on the curb watching me drive away."

The image of how he described me made me feel a twinge of embarrassment, even though I knew part of him enjoyed knowing that his departure had turned me into an emotional wreck. "I'm fine," I casually said. "I stopped crying."

"I figured you would—eventually," he chuckled.

We were both aware that the phone call was costly, so we kept it brief and made plans for our next call. I reminded him about my upcoming college move-in schedule, which I could tell made him feel vulnerable. He wasn't the only one experiencing college life, partying, and meeting people. Before concluding with "love you," he reasserted his earlier promise: "Remember—I'm going to write to you regularly. You'll see!"

Mark's word was good—better than that, in fact. To say he was prolific would be an understatement. The cards and letters poured into my mailbox within a few days. Sometimes he scribbled notes on sheets of paper, other times he took time and care to send greeting cards, which alternated among funny, corny, romantic, and sentimental. All of them were heartfelt. I could tell he was deliberate in his card selections and word choices in the notes themselves, even when they had to be rushed.

[undated, Fall 1986]

Dear Juliette,
No sunset is complete without you.

Love,
Mark

Sometimes he would use his fancy dot matrix printer to creatively generate a message.

[undated, Fall 1986]

Juliette,
    My one & only.

        I LOVE U

                Love,
                Mark

I replied to Mark as often as I could, but I admit I couldn't possibly keep up with him—especially when I started packing for college. That seemed to be all right by him. He knew he was an overachiever on this front and seemed happy when I found the time to correspond back. I was almost always available for him by phone when he called and, although we had to be money conscious about our phone bills, we made sure this was quality time.

Meanwhile, I was growing increasingly concerned that my dorm situation hadn't been settled. Since my parents' house was in such proximity to the college, I was lower on the totem pole for a room than others who resided farther away. I was placed on hold until after classes started because everything had filled up. I had to wait and commute to classes until something happened to become available. By the time I received a room assignment a week later, everyone else had already moved in, and I was behind in terms of getting to know people.

I had high expectations of my roommate and hoped we'd hit it off and become friends. The tall, skinny brunette frowned the moment I stepped foot in our room. "Great," she sighed, before I even had a chance to introduce myself. "I have a roommate."

That was a clear indication that a friendship was not going to happen. We were total opposites: Whereas I was a typical middle-class Long Island girl who applied hair product and makeup (although not nearly as much as others I knew), Ivy was a full-fledged Deadhead with zero cosmetics and a wardrobe consisting exclusively of tie-dyed T-shirts and frayed jeans. It didn't take long for me to identify the vegetation by the window as pot plants and take notice of the pharmaceuticals jammed into our shared fridge, which didn't even allow any room for my one yogurt container. Predictably, the wall above her bed displayed skeletal Grateful Dead posters, concert paraphernalia, and psychedelic imagery.

I had nothing against any of this and tried to avoid coming across as judgmental. The courtesy wasn't reciprocated, however. As soon as I was about to hang up my 1980s "girlie" teen posters of Madonna and champagne bottles of spurting bubbles, she gasped, "Are you *sure* you want to hang up that stuff?" My tastes cramped her style from the get-go, and her chilly attitude toward me never warmed. We ended up avoiding each other throughout the semester, which was just as well. I had Mark and more than enough friends from back home to help me feel confident that I would eventually find my own friend group.

I called Mark right away, inserting multiple coins into a pay phone by the dorm entrance. When he asked how things were going, I assured him everything was great and didn't mention my sourpuss roommate, as I didn't want him to be concerned and couldn't risk anyone overhearing me openly trash-talking someone on my first day. We worked out a phone schedule when we were certain we'd both be around.

I missed Mark but had plenty of things going on to keep myself occupied. In addition to visits from old friends who were attending colleges nearby, I made a few new friends at Hofstra, including Carrie, who had a single room in our shared suite. She was funny and welcoming, although other girls considered her "weird." She had a reptile collection and snuck one of her "babies"—a giant iguana named Zeus—into school. To my knowledge, she never got caught with it.

I admit I was not a great student at the time. I wasn't invested, hoping to skate through the academics and enjoy everything else. I dropped and switched classes around left and right. Although I declared a theater major, my dad protested right away: "There's no way I'm paying for that!" He made my life difficult, pushing me into going for a BA instead of a BFA, which required taking math and science classes. I signed up for the easiest math class they had to offer. When I found myself struggling, I showed up at my professor's office hours in a panic. "I'm a drama major, there's no way I'm going to pass this class."

"Don't worry, you'll pass," he reassured me with hints of pity and condescension.

To my surprise, I *did* pass. It seemed to do the trick getting my dad off my back, and I never had to suffer through another math class again.

I did my own thing in college, diving headfirst in campus activities. I auditioned for all the plays and musicals. I didn't tell anyone at school that I also entered the Miss Long Island Pageant, the local pageant for the Miss America franchise. It sounds strange, in retrospect, because the contest seemed so old-fashioned even by 1980s standards, but I was lured in by the $2,500 prize money (plus a watch)—which would have been a big help toward paying tuition and housing. I convinced myself I had a real shot at winning this because talent was half the criteria, and I knew I could sing well. Between entrance fees and my wardrobe, it ended up being more expensive than I had anticipated, but I qualified for the preliminaries of the New York State Pageant and managed to take third runner-up and make the local newspaper. *Not bad*, I thought, even though I didn't earn back my investment.

It ended up being a long stretch until I saw Mark again. The ride back and forth was too long for either of us, especially during the winter amidst bad weather. The distance caused me to occasionally wonder whether we should see other people. I wanted to fully experience college, so I was conflicted. I kept my options open, but not once considered breaking up with Mark. I was always honest with him, telling him when I was going to a party or formal with someone else. I also made it clear that I was not looking to "replace" him. He seemed agitated and jealous every time I mentioned my social activities, but he never put his foot down. He continued to display a high level of maturity, recognizing there was nothing he could do to control what I did at college and that he was unwilling to lose what we had together.

At the end of the day, his patience paid off, as it gave me the chance to decide for myself that no one else compared with him. More often than not, I found myself telling new friends and classmates "I have a boyfriend in Albany."

Meanwhile, his cards and letters kept coming. I cherished every single one. Some of Mark's favorites were the humorous Sandra Boynton cards. One particular one had a sad-looking cartoon beaver holding some logs of wood on the front. The blurb said, "I'm sorry I haven't had time to write..." while the inside had the words "... but it's just been one dam project after another." Mark loved those corny puns!

[undated, Fall 1986]

Dear Juliette,
You know I always have you on my mind. Maybe that's why I never get anything done. I'm just so fucking busy.
but it's just been one dam project after another.
But I always think of you because I need you.

Love,
Mark

We saw each other again during breaks around Thanksgiving and Christmas. Our romance picked up right where it left off, but our time together always seemed to end too soon. When we returned to our respective campuses, the cards and letters resumed, flooding my mailbox throughout the school year. Each one seemed more intimate than the one before.

[undated, February 1987]

Dear Juliette,
Yes, I do need you. You are my hope, my dreams, my love. When I am not with you, I am incomplete.

I NEED YOU!
BE MY VALENTINE!

Love,
Mark

Mark was especially attentive when it came to remembering birthdays, anniversaries, and other special events. The gifts, cards, and letters usually showed up early, and he always called on those days as well.

[undated, April 1987]

Can you believe it all began one night at the Spit club? How old are you anyway? It has been a great nine months. (WOW—that long!) Anyway, happy birthday and happy anniversary.
    From a man who constantly thinks of you.

Love,
Mark

As it happened, I only spent one semester on campus. The drive to Hofstra wasn't that bad and housing wasn't worth the inflated cost. My life didn't change all that much, especially with Mark remaining a constant. He put his heart and soul into every correspondence.

[undated, August 1987]

Dear Juliette,
Yes, it is true, I do love you, more than you can imagine. It has been a year since I "forced" you into a decision . . . and each day I am happier I did so. I do not know what I would have done this past year without you, and the thought of losing you to someone else kills me. I'll do anything to keep you for you are my "baby," and I need you. You are my love, my honey, and probably my best friend. Always remember that, for nothing can change the way I feel or how much I love you.

Love,
Mark

Mark sent me another humorous Sarah Boynton greeting card. This time there was a cartoon figure of the Abominable Snowman on a snowdrift on the front, along with the words "Without you..." When you opened the card, you saw the punchline.

[undated, circa 1987]

Dear Juliette,
Exactly two weeks till I'm home again.
Exactly two weeks till I see you again.
Exactly two weeks of missing you and two weeks left of waiting to see you.
I feel Abominable.
Until those two weeks end.

Love,
Mark

[undated, circa 1988]

Dear Jules,
I had a great time with you this weekend. The more time I spend with you, the more I miss you when I'm away at school. I really wish you were here with me. What fun we would have! It would be great to walk to class with you, eat dinner with you, and spend all of my time with you.
  Where would I be without you?

Love,
Mark

[undated, circa 1988]

Dear Juliette,
Did I tell you how much I love you? Have I told you lately? If I have not, kick me for neglecting you!
I love you more than I can say. You are my best friend, the one I lean on, the one I depend on. You cheer me up when I'm sad, entertain me

when I'm bored, hug me when I need a hug. You are everything to me and the perfect woman.

Too often, the word love is thrown around. People "love" sports, say they "love" ice cream (I know I am one of them)... but few say "I love you" and mean it. I do love you and I do mean it. <u>Always love me back!</u>

Love,
Mark

[undated, circa August 1988]

I love you
I cannot believe it has been two years. The time I spend with you has gone so quickly that I can never think enough of you.

Love,
Mark

October 27, 1988

Dear Juliette,
Hi Baby, what's up? Right now, I'm sitting in Management, and we are watching a film. Boy is this class ever boring. How is my Honey-Bunny? God, I miss you. I keep thinking of you and when I'm going to see you again.

Yesterday was my last mid-term, for at least three weeks. Thank God that is over. I did poorly only on one test (I think). I got a 74 on this Management test. That should curve to a B. All others should be all right. So last night, Neil and I went out on the town. It felt great to go out. But my thoughts were only of you. I can't remember the last time I went out, and I can't remember the last time I did not think of you. This is very bad. I am always thinking of you.

Nothing else is really up. Now that my tests are over, I have to catch up on all of my readings. I have fallen a little behind, but I have so many other things happening. There are the pledges I have to take care of. Plus, this Saturday my fraternity is hosting a Halloween party. This should be fun because I get to play Bouncer.

Yesterday, I had to make up my schedule for next semester. This is the last time I have to register for classes and that is one headache that I never have to deal with again. It took fucking forever. But the schedule I have is not the best, but it is pretty good. I have no classes on Monday and Friday and only one class on Wednesday.

I will be coming home on November 3 for the weekend, so leave time for me.

Until I speak to you again,
My thoughts are only of you.

Love,
Mark

We made it intact as a couple through those four years without a single issue. By the time I graduated, I knew I couldn't live without him. I had finally "caught up" to him in terms of maturity and understanding what I wanted in a partner. Mark had all those qualities. There was simply no resisting the fact that we were both deeply and passionately in love.

Chapter Eight

A Ring and a Reunion

New York, New York
Fall 1989–Fall 1993

Mark's life kicked in gear, as planned. Toward the end of his senior year, he applied to top law schools and was accepted at several, including the University of Chicago, which tempted him with a bundle of scholarship money. Due to its proximity to Long Island, NYU School of Law ended up being his final choice. He wanted to be near his family—and to me. Instead of our long-distance romance in which we were connected by love letters and expensive phone calls, we suddenly had access to each other via an easy ride on the Long Island Railroad and the A and E subway lines.

Mark moved into a two-bedroom apartment with a shared kitchen and bathroom in D'Agostino Hall, the brand-new NYU law dorm. Located on West Third Street and MacDougal, it was a prime spot for both of us. On weekends—and even some weeknights when I didn't have class—we could explore Greenwich Village and roam the city together. Our activities always had to be on the cheap because neither of us had much money. Sometimes we'd venture to Broadway to see what bargains we could find at Odd Job discount store. At night, we'd occasionally splurge on sushi and then head off to an inexpensive bar, dance club, or comedy club.

Not only did Mark luck out being housed in a modern new building closely situated to everything, but he also had the good fortune of landing the perfect roommate: Richard (Rick) Levy, a first-year law student from Westchester, New York. The two couldn't have been a better fit. Both were immaculate and studious and kept their dorm squeaky clean. They became fast friends, working out together and bulking up their slender frames with protein powder. The third "roommate" was Rick's pet, Bandit, a friendly ferret with only one fang. Despite the reputation ferrets have for fouling up homes, Rick and Mark managed to keep their apartment so tidy and odor-free one might never know Bandit resided with them. If she'd been exposed, Bandit would most certainly have gotten the boot.

Rick didn't mind when I stayed over a couple weekends or so out of the month or occasionally crashed there on a weeknight if I happened to have an acting audition in the city.

I felt fortunate to have found a talent agent who was willing to work with me, although he made it clear he didn't think much of my prospects, remarking that a national commercial I had been booked was a result of "sheer luck." My confidence was shaky when I found myself reading for a senior casting director for a new role on the *General Hospital* television soap opera as Tony Geary's sister. "You look enough like the actor" offered my agent. Realizing I had prepared and rehearsed with a few missing lines, I panicked and blew my chances. After that, I found myself at nontraditional auditions, such as a young female MC at a monster truck rally.

Mark was supportive throughout. At night, we would lie in his cramped twin-sized bed and share our experiences from that day. We laughed about how ridiculous we must have looked in that bed—especially since Mark was so tall—but we enjoyed sharing such intimate space together. He listened intently as I filled him in on the highs and lows of my acting career.

We had to be scrappy when it came to feeding ourselves, since Mark didn't have a meal plan. Fortunately, he was self-sufficient and knew how to cook a few basic dishes. At the time, I was hapless in the kitchen; the extent of my culinary knowledge was popping a Lean Cuisine in the microwave. I was grateful when Mark taught me how to prepare some simple things, such as scrambled eggs and stir-fry chicken dishes.

His first year successfully completed, Mark landed his first summer associate job at a prestigious Manhattan law firm. He received favorable feedback and encouragement, and was under the distinct impression that summer associates were offered full-time employment after graduation unless they had messed up or there was some other unforeseen disaster. He was shocked and disappointed when this did not transpire. He speculated that someone at the firm regarded him as overconfident and as a potential threat, or else there existed some sort of personality clash. No matter the case, out of concern for his financial situation and due to his sense of pride, he jumped right back into the interview process.

Mark became more panicked as his second year of law school drew to a close without a serious prospect. He desperately needed to secure a job before graduation.

At last, an opportunity opened for him in the Bronx DA's office. He had to work hard to convince them that he was the right fit. They took one look at his background and pegged him as someone with ambitions in litigation and "big law" (which was the case). They took a chance on him, however, which ended up working out all around. Mark accepted a job as an assistant district attorney. He loved the hands-on experience the role afforded him. He also found the work interesting and respected the work ethic and passion of his colleagues. He might have remained there forever, except for two related issues: they required a three-year commitment, and the pay was crap. With tens of thousands of dollars in loans to pay back, $40,000 per year wasn't going to cut it. He saw the job as a stepping-stone to greater things.

As my relationship with Mark blossomed, our families gradually became more intertwined. I became privy to many things that went on in his family, as his parents officially divorced.

The beloved family home in Merrick—and its years filled with memories—was sold, and Mrs. Brisman moved to a more manageable two-bedroom apartment with a den in Bayside, Queens.

She didn't arrive at her new home completely alone, however; a neurotic Shih Tzu, Theodore E. Bear—Theo for short—was always by her side. He was an adorable purebred, but high maintenance. He had to be coaxed into doing anything—even eating and going for walks.

Since the twins were students in the New York area—Michelle was going for her doctorate degree—they made their mother's apartment home, taking turns staying there with her and Theo. But the building had peculiar rules against dog ownership—only those who already had a canine could be "grandfathered in" to adopt one or get a replacement—which meant we (Mark, Michelle, and/or I) had to sneak the dog in and out in a gym bag. When someone in the building became suspicious, a kind neighbor offered to pretend that she owned Theo and say that the twins were just his dog walkers. Due to the Shih Tzu's numerous idiosyncrasies, I privately took to referring to him as "Shithead"—or *SH* for short—since I had a love/hate relationship with him.

As the years went by, Mark and I were more frequently invited as plus-ones to each other's family events, such as cousins' weddings. We began to discuss our future together and presented ourselves as a committed couple. It was only a matter of time before would be ready to share our long-term plans with our respective families.

Unbeknownst to me at the time, Mark had purchased an engagement ring, and on Valentine's Day, he set the stage for a romantic dinner at One if by Land, Two if by Sea on Barrow Street in New York City. My suspicions had been raised because it was a pricey restaurant for a Valentine's Day celebration. As soon as we sat down, I asked, "Is this some kind of special surprise'? If it is, just tell me now. I'm too excited. I won't be able to relax and enjoy the evening!"

"Do you really think I would take a diamond ring into the subway all across the city to propose to you?" he quipped, as if the suggestion defied logic.

I considered his words. There was nothing suspicious about his appearance. He had come straight from work in his usual suit and overcoat, briefcase in hand. Mark was practical, and I doubted he would chance a ring being lost or stolen by taking the subway. I was more relieved than disappointed, as I didn't want or need to be the center of attention in an expensive restaurant. I could simply enjoy a wonderful dinner in a magical setting. "That's true," I relented.

I chatted away as the evening progressed through delicious drinks, appetizers, and main courses. Mark seemed a bit on the quiet side. I chalked it up to a long day at work and the chaos of a bustling, upscale restaurant. He wasn't the type of guy who perspired much, but his face seemed to be doused with sweat and his hand felt clammy when he reached over to hold mine.

The smirking waiter danced to our table and asked, "Are you ready for dessert?"

"Yes, thank you," Mark replied before I had a chance to chime in.

What's the rush?

I agreed to look at our options on the menu and ordered.

We became uncharacteristically silent as we waited for dessert to arrive. Mark's eyes darted to and from the kitchen area. A few minutes later, an entourage led by our waiter swept to our table with a covered silver tray. When he had our full attention, he placed it at the center of the table. He removed the domed lid in what seemed to be slow motion. My eyes widened as he revealed a bed of red rose petals with a magnificent diamond ring sparkling in the center.

As Mark went down on one knee, all eyes in the restaurant fastened on us. My body tingled with excitement. I couldn't have been more surprised that this was happening. "I love you, Juliette . . . will you marry me?" he proposed.

My heart leapt for joy hearing the words aloud. I'd never felt such love for another person. Overcome with emotion, I whispered through my tears, "Yes."

We kissed and then he slid the ring on my finger. I stared at it, frozen, while uttering "Wow, just wow!" The restaurant's patrons and staff gave us a standing ovation. We were grand Valentine's Day entertainment. Mark laughed—an emotional release that his plan had been well-executed and successfully accomplished, despite my having posed some early challenges for him. I don't recall what the dessert was or if we even bothered to taste it. I was walking on clouds. I'd agreed to marry the man I would pledge myself to for the rest of our lives.

I didn't question Mark about the cost of the ring, but I knew it was expensive and he couldn't have afforded it on his own. As it happened, the funding came from a surprising source: his father.

They'd reconnected when Mark heard that his grandmother—his

father's mother—had passed away. He didn't want to miss the funeral—especially when he happened to hear Harry Chapin's song "Cat's in the Cradle" on the radio. Despite the awkwardness of not seeing his father for a while, he wanted to attend the service. "It's the right thing to do," he said. Given the unusual circumstances and the fact that I didn't know his grandmother, we decided it was best if I didn't attend.

When Mark arrived to pay his respects, Mr. Brisman didn't recognize him at first. They hadn't seen each other in a while, during which time Mark had changed dramatically in appearance, and looked more mature. Mr. Brisman was pleased and excited that Mark had made an effort to come. It marked a new beginning for their relationship. Mark was introduced to Eva, his father's wife. The three of them made a point of agreeing to stay in touch and make plans to see each other. Mr. Brisman expressed interest in meeting me, too—properly this time.

Mark and his father kept their word and made plans for the four of us. The funeral paved the way for that to happen. If Mark wanted a better relationship with his father, I intended to support his choice.

It started out with dinner at a fine restaurant in Manhattan. Both Mr. Brisman and the second Mrs. Brisman affectionately welcomed us as soon as we saw them. While she was predictably blonde, attractive, and young in comparison to Mark's father, she was a kind, pleasant person. She sincerely wanted to get to know us.

We caught up on lost time by filling them in on our lives and careers: Mr. Brisman's publishing business, Mark's law career, my post-college plans, and so on. We shared stories, told jokes, and laughed the rest of the evening. They were charming and we enjoyed each other's company. Mr. Brisman treated us for the dinner, which was a good thing because we couldn't have afforded it.

I felt happy for Mark. He had found what he so needed and

wanted.

A closer relationship with his father.

This was only the first of many get-togethers among the four of us. Mr. Brisman took us to several more wonderful restaurants, as well as Broadway shows. The two seemed determined to make up for lost time.

Sadly, the reconnection was bittersweet. For reasons too private to reveal, it was decided that Jerry and Eva would not attend our upcoming wedding.

Chapter Nine

Wedding Bells

Temple Torah
Little Neck, New York
November 6, 1993

In the weeks before our wedding, Mark and I initiated putting the pieces of our lives together. This was the real deal: cohabitation in our first home.

Mark found an apartment in the Boulevard Apartments on Corporal Kennedy Street in Bayside, Queens, that (not uncoincidentally) was located directly across the street from his mother's residence. Mark and I began to feel a certain amount of responsibility for my future mother-in-law since we were in closest proximity and were concerned about how she would manage if we were to move too far away. He came and went to see her with such frequency that the building doormen assumed he was still a resident and gave him carte blanche to come and go as he pleased.

Mark adroitly juggled being a good son and a loving husband. He took the free shuttle—available only to "residents" of her apartment—from the train station, which was close by her building. On returning from the city, Mark would go to his mother's apartment, chat with her, and walk Theo. Afterward, he'd head home in plenty of time for our private dinner for two across the street.

Our apartment was special not only because it was our first home together but because it also marked an official separation from my living at home with my parents. I'd only lived outside of East Meadow during that one brief semester of my freshman year and during short stints for work. I played it matter-of-factly, informing my parents that I was moving out just before I started to pack my things. My mother took it as a big deal, however, exclaiming, "What do you mean, you're moving *so soon*?!" Ultimately, she found a way to deal with her first born leaving the nest.

Our six-story building, located right by the Throggs Neck Bridge, was nothing fancy. It struck me as a mix of older folks and younger people just starting out. Parking was outside the building and our "security" consisted of a lone guard in a jeep patrolling the exterior of several buildings until his shift ended for the day. This didn't prevent hubcap thievery, which was so common that Mark and I never had any on our tires, as they would have been removed overnight.

Unlike my mother-in-law's building, ours did not have a doorman. People had to get buzzed in by a tenant. The lobby had a speckled tile floor with a big round cushioned piece of furniture in the center for sitting. Lining the area were frosted glass mirrors to give the appearance of a much larger space. An update was sorely needed, but the residents didn't seem to mind.

The rent for our fourth-floor, one-bedroom apartment was $900 a month, which wasn't such a bargain back in 1993. For me, the new environment was something of a wake-up call. I relished the idea of being independent from my parents and starting my life with Mark, but our urban dwelling was a radical change from the house in the suburbs: the L-shaped design with a pass-through kitchen, the small square footage, the lack of outdoor breathing space, and the one shared bathroom. The metal safety grates on the windows gave me pause. I wondered whether they were there to prevent children or pets from falling out the window, to deter thieves from finding a way inside our apartment, or both. I was thrilled that the owner of the unit—a woman who was moving into a new place with her boyfriend—offered us her hand-me-down dining set, a massive wooden table with chairs that had brown-and-cream-striped velour upholstery and woven lattice backing. Not exactly stylish, but sturdy and one less expense to worry about. We did purchase an off-white sleeper sofa and loveseat with slightly shiny fabric from Jennifer Convertibles. The color was risky, I thought, but a welcome departure from the dark pattern fabrics in my childhood home. A collection of jointly purchased teddy bears added a personal touch. Cream lacy curtains in a romantic style and floral throw pillows completed the look.

It took a while for me to feel safe there, even though Mark changed the locks on the front door the instant we moved in. On one occasion while I was home alone, Mark told me the building super was going to stop by to make a minor repair in the bathroom. He knocked repeatedly but didn't say who he was—and I was too timid to look through the peephole—so I pretended I wasn't home. He gave up and left. Mark was none too happy with me until I admitted that I was too nervous to answer the door.

There were some other adjustments. While I was aware Mark was something of a neat freak who liked everything just so, I was unprepared for living with a person like that. Everything had to be in the right place. His clothing was either neatly folded or hung up; nothing touched the floor or was strewn carelessly. Although I wasn't especially messy, I felt I had to up my game and develop positive habits of always leaving shoes at the door and hanging up my coat in the hall closet.

I was untrained as a homemaker, since my mother had insisted on doing all the domestic work while I was growing up. My father did little in the kitchen. When I moved in with Mark, I assumed the home was my domain and made some poor attempts at emulating my mother's role. When I loaded the dishwasher, Mark would emphatically shake his head and say, "That's not how you do it" and redo the position of every plate, bowl, glass, and utensil. He never had a negative or mean tone; he was just stating a fact. I bristled, of course, because I thought he was being critical of me and that he was invading my turf.

Eventually, I improved at chores and became less sensitive about his involvement in them. I even grew to appreciate it. Who wouldn't be happy with a spouse who didn't mind cleaning?

Early on, I learned how to cook and made most of our dinners. I started out with casserole-type one-dish meals I'd picked up from my mother, but they didn't cut it for Mark. He was a red meat and potatoes kind of guy and preferred this to fish or vegetarian meals. Fortunately, I made a mean chicken soup that satisfied both of us. Outside of that, I had to do an about-face and prepare steak or lamb chops. In the beginning, I was too intimidated to try to cook an entire chicken or roast beef. He didn't mind when I snuck in a green vegetable and/or a salad with his meat and potatoes. Once I knew what to cook, Mark wasn't picky, and thankfully, he devoured everything on his plate.

Mark was a traditional kind of guy and saw himself in the future as the breadwinner with a wife at home to manage things. Given all his massive school loans and our newfound expenses, we both realized right away that an old-fashioned husband/wife dynamic wasn't going to happen—at least not right away.

I had no issue with placing my acting career on hiatus to help our financial situation. Instead of going to auditions, I took a full-time job as assistant store manager at the newly opening Lane Bryant plus-sized store at The Bay Terrace Shopping Center, the mall around the corner from our apartment. I didn't feel the least bit frustrated with the decision to take on a full-time job; it was a small sacrifice I was willing to make.

Even so, Mark vowed, "This won't be forever," reaffirming his long-range goal of a suburban paradise with me in the role of stay-at-home mom.

The job was the perfect fit for me. I liked fashion and found I had something of a knack for selling clothing, probably because I enjoyed helping other women look their best and was interested in hearing them talk about their lives. After a while, I had my regular customers who relied on my assistance and "expert" opinion.

Mark and I maneuvered our way through the holidays by dividing our time between both sides of the family. On the Jewish High Holidays—Rosh Hashanah and Yom Kippur—we would attend The Bay Terrace Synagogue in Queens with Mrs. Brisman. In the evening, we'd have dinners with my parents and assorted aunts, uncles, cousins, and my grandmother. Thanksgiving was always spent at the home of a relative on my side of the family.

Mark appreciated my parents and got along well with them—as was also true with the rest of my extended family—although he sometimes considered my parents' well-intentioned involvement in our affairs a bit smothering. He joked that things would always run smoothly, as long as there was a "bridge" in between our respective homes, alluding to certain boundaries remaining intact.

The wedding was set for November 6, 1993, a Saturday evening, at Temple Torah in Little Neck, New York. It was a beautiful Conservative synagogue surrounded by well-manicured, lush greenery—lawn, bushes, and trees—even though fall was well underway. By Long Island standards, it was a medium-sized wedding, with about 150 attendees. We had all the trimmings of a grand affair with ice sculptures, flowers, and decorations everywhere you turned and a full live pop/rock band that performed all the standards of the time. My parents insisted on the event being handled by a kosher caterer, which was seen as the right thing to do, even though neither of our families practiced the laws of kashrut. The proceedings began with a Havdalah (end of Shabbat) service, followed by a cocktail hour with tons of food. We had to have "everything."

We had a somewhat large bridal party, consisting of our siblings and several friends. The women wore jewel-tone long gowns in shades of plum or emerald. The men were dressed in classic formal tuxedos. My sister served as the maid of honor, while Steven was Mark's best man. Mrs. Brisman—who would forever-after become known to me as Roberta—stood by her son's side to start the procession in a beaded black and white formal gown, while my parents escorted me down the aisle to the accompaniment of classical music in matching black-and-white formal attire. I dressed to impress in a white, long-sleeve, heavily beaded gown with a full tulle skirt; my hair was styled in an elaborate updo, and a long veil trailed behind me. Although my feet were concealed, my shoes were gold fabric designer heels that had been repurposed from a prior affair, plucked from the clearance rack at Saks. Mark seemed happy and focused on the moment, not appearing to be nervous.

The rabbi led the service, after which Mark and I recited our vows and kissed. We were declared husband and wife, and pranced hand-in-hand back down the aisle to the sound of upbeat Jewish music and clapping.

Everything went without a hitch—well, *almost* everything. Unbeknownst to Mark and everyone else, I was sick to my stomach the entire day. I didn't know if it was nerves or a stomach flu, but I felt increasingly horrible as the day progressed. My tight wedding gown, which had been taken in quite a bit, didn't help matters.

The band leader introduced "Mr. and Mrs. Mark Brisman" and out we came, all smiles and song. Somehow, I managed to hold down whatever was in my stomach as the band launched into the hora. Everyone hopped onto the dance floor and joined hands to form one small circle and several wider circles around us. We danced and clapped until two chairs were brought out. Mark and I were raised up high, bobbing and weaving in the air. Lord only knows what I looked like up there, as the queasy feeling in my belly lurched upward to my throat.

Miraculously, I held off just long enough. When the music ended and the crowd dispersed, I scurried out of the room in an overwhelmed daze, grabbing my sister on the way out. We retreated to the bathroom, where I flung open a stall door, knelt, and promptly threw up in the bowl. To my amazement, I didn't get a single stain on my dress. I also couldn't believe my good fortune that no one else was in the bathroom to see or hear me.

I returned to the party as if nothing had happened, although I'm sure my face looked pale and sallow. There was no way I was going to worry anyone or ruin the celebration—especially for Mark, who was walking on air. I took my seat next to him at the dais—a private table set for two—numb to everything around me. It felt good to finally relax and not have to *do* anything—at least for a while. I didn't eat a single morsel or drink anything except water throughout the entire wedding.

I pulled myself together enough to get back on my feet for my first dance with Mark to the song "You're Too Good to Be True." I felt myself sink into his arms to reserve my strength. I must have put on a great performance, as no signs of how I felt were visible in the wedding photographs.

The party ramped up. For whatever reason—maybe because friends and relatives in their twenties and thirties didn't have children yet—a lot of people got crazy drunk. Fortunately, no one ended up getting too rowdy. I watched this with simultaneous pleasure (that our wedding was a hit) and annoyance (questioning the decision to have an open bar).

After we cut the wedding cake and dessert was served, I only had one remaining obligation left: throwing the bouquet. I turned my back to the swarm of women ages eighteen to sixty and threw the bunch of flowers over my head behind me. I could hear the stampede charge after it. My dad's eccentric middle-aged cousin came up with the prize.

I couldn't wait to get out of there and yank off that dress. We stuck to our plan of returning to our Queens apartment, arriving home at two in the morning. I have no idea why we had thought it was a good idea to fly from JFK for our honeymoon at five that same morning. As soon as the dress was off and I'd plunked on the bed, we had to get right back up, finish packing, and head for the airport.

Mark, who was still on a high from the wedding (but not hungover), kept us on track and ensured we made it to the gate on time. I felt miserable and exhausted. "Oh why did we do this?" I groaned, not really expecting an answer.

"Don't worry," Mark assured me. "You'll have plenty of time to rest once we're at the hotel in Jamaica."

He was right. Things turned around as soon as we lifted off. I slept on the short flight and was able to nap even after landing and settling in our room at the Sandals Ocho Rios. I could finally relax and acknowledge that it had all really happened: We were married. I didn't have any second thoughts. I loved Mark and knew he was the right man for me.

Our honeymoon was fantastic. We had an all-inclusive package and our pick of the hotel restaurants. Not that this meant much to me; my stomach was still weak, and I mostly stuck to consuming the lush fresh fruits.

This Sandals hotel served couples only, so there were no loud children under our feet. We met a bunch of other pleasant honeymooners and did all the couple activities, including climbing up

Dunn's River Falls. More precisely, Mark and a local guide hauled me up the slippery rock wall.

Toward the end of our vacation, we attended an outdoor market. It was fun browsing through the island's wares and novelty items. At one stand, an object called out to me: a wooden trinket that looked like an elaborately carved whistle. I thought it was cool and decided I wanted it. Mark dutifully bought it for me. As we walked away from the vendor's booth, a man approached and whispered something in Mark's ear. He smiled widely as soon as the man stepped away.

"What is it?" I asked. "What's so funny?"

"Do you realize what you just bought?" he chuckled.

I examined it closer and drew a blank. "What is it, then?"

"A pot pipe. The guy was trying to make his own sale."

I joined him in the laughter. My one keepsake from our honeymoon was an inexpensive Jamaican pot pipe. I wondered if and when it would ever come in handy.

Chapter Ten

Baby Brismans

Bayside, Queens
December 1993–May 1998

As Mark and I started our married life together, we adhered to our tight budget, which meant we didn't venture out much outside of Queens or live it up as newlyweds. When I didn't prepare dinner, we'd explore the local ethnic cuisine on Bayside's Bell Boulevard—especially Chinese and Japanese sushi restaurants, which were quite good—but, for the most part, we'd end up at affordable places such as Uno's Pizza or the local diner. Our big nights out on weekends meant attending the seemingly never-ending conveyer belt of weddings. We were at that age when it seemed as if all our high school friends, college friends, and coworkers were tying the knot at the same time.

Meanwhile, Mark and I were already gearing up for the next stage: starting a family. The subject of having a baby came up often. When Mark worried we weren't ready, I'd pose the question, "When is anyone ever ready?"

"Good point," he said.

"But what if we can't have children?" I asked.

"I don't know," he replied. "Let's hope it doesn't come to that. I'm not adopting."

I was surprised at the definitiveness of his comment because, at the time, I had no strong opinion on the topic one way or another. I let it go, assuming we'd reopen the conversation later, if need be.

We knew other couples who were having fertility issues and mutually arrived at the conclusion that if it was going to take five years for us to conceive, we should at least start exploring the idea. So . . . we got busy exploring.

For ten months, we discarded one negative pregnancy test after the other. Our hope for a spring baby dimmed. We both wondered what issue was causing it to take so long.

Then I noticed my period was a bit late, and, once again, I opened a store-bought pregnancy test kit. Mark and I looked at the result together. We couldn't believe it . . . *positive*!

We immediately contacted my OB/GYN office for an appointment and were promptly declined. They told me it was premature to do the official test; we'd have to come in weeks later when I was farther along. We knew I was pregnant, but it's just not the same thing as hearing it from a doctor. Somehow, we made it through the pregnancy protocol of waiting, after which we finally had the pregnancy confirmed at the OB/GYN's office. Baby Brisman was due to arrive on December 6.

Almost immediately afterward, I was hammered by the usual symptoms and signs. I felt *terrible*, suffering from nasty morning sickness and having aversions to chicken and meat. At the same time, my appetite exploded, and I was always hungry, seeking anything that fit into my newly adopted vegetarian (although far from low calorie) diet. I started gaining weight right away—too much, I supposed. One of my preferred outings was going with Roberta to Sizzler's all-you-can-eat salad bar lunch buffet.

I stopped working at the clothing store halfway into my fifth month, as I was already heavily showing and didn't want to buy an entire maternity wardrobe. My employer didn't seem the least bit surprised when I quit.

I had plenty of nesting to do at home to keep me occupied. Roberta was excited to get involved and bought the layette and other newborn firsts. I was glad we were able to bond over this. Not to be outdone, my parents laid claim on the crib and furnishings. Otherwise, we didn't receive many gifts from the baby registry until later. Many Jewish families (at least at the time) tended to be superstitious about putting the "evil eye" on familial circumstances. The theory was that buying baby stuff prior to birth would cause bad luck to the child or family. For this reason, I didn't have a baby shower.

Somehow, I became convinced we were going to have a boy. I even dreamt about giving birth to a son. Mark and I picked out an assortment of boy's names based on the tradition of paying respect to deceased family members. We both agreed we wanted to find out the gender, so we told the technician who conducted the sonogram and ultrasound to inform us. Unfortunately, after numerous angles and retries, the technician admitted defeat. "The baby is being stubborn and won't allow me a clear look," she joked. We would simply have to wait.

What a cute story to tell my son someday . . .

The remaining months of my pregnancy, once the nausea subsided, were mostly easy and uneventful. As we counted down the final days to the due date, I started to feel "something" and called the medical office to find if it was time to come in. They gave some suggestions on how to time the contractions and what it would feel like when it was getting serious. We were close . . . but not there yet.

December 4, 1996, two days before the due date: I'd had enough. I had spent much of the night sitting at the kitchen table with my head on the tabletop to rest before being jolted awake by a contraction. Mark sat nearby, helplessly staring at his stopwatch. He called the medical office the next time to plead my case. Next thing I knew, we were heading to the car, an overnight bag in hand.

I arrived at North Shore Hospital. They had me fill out the paperwork and go through an examination. Sure enough, I wasn't ready. They refused to check me in. I shuffled around the hallways for quite a while, hoping my status would progress—or that the staff would change their minds. No dice. "You're not ready," the nurse said. "You still have time. Go home."

Mark drove me home. A short time later, it became clear the contractions were timed right. We had to reverse course back to North Shore, where I was greeted by a familiar face who blurted, "You still haven't had that baby yet?!" A doctor finally made the call I was waiting for and said, "Let's help you out here and move this along."

At last, things were proceeding at a rapid pace. I was checked in and administered Pitosin. Then an epidural. One of the nurses reassured me, "You're going to have this baby soon."

Then we waited. Nothing happened. I became frustrated because my doctor was not there, apparently unavailable. A nurse whose name eludes me (and I'd sooner forget) without any detectable bedside manner was left to tend to me. She ordered me to start pushing, so I pushed. She commanded me to try harder and gave all kinds of directions that I attempted to follow. "What's the problem?" she demanded. "You're not doing it right."

Not doing it right? This clearly isn't her first baby—but it is mine!

As time progressed without any progress, she became increasingly miffed at me. When the OB/GYN poked his head in from time to time, she'd huff, "No, not yet." Clearly, this was all my fault. I was already a bad mother, and the child hadn't even entered this world yet.

Hours passed. My power struggle with the nurse raged. "You have to try harder!"

"I *can't*," I whimpered. "I'm exhausted. I have nothing left."

She threw up her hands. Then the doctor threw up his hands. I'd find out later that doctors hated doing C-sections because they were under pressure not to. This one apparently didn't want my low-risk case to mess with his quota.

"Prep her and wheel her in," he commanded, as if I were a cowardly soldier being forced into rejoining a losing battle.

C-section. Finally.

Mark and I were led into a prep room. I couldn't have felt more relieved that this was at last going to be over. They pulled a curtain across my chest to shield my eyes from what was about to commence. A nurse from the team took my hand and spoke softly to me throughout, using his calm voice to comfort and distract me.

Suddenly, someone in the room shouted, "*It's a girl!*"

"Are you *sure?*" I asked.

"Yeah, we're sure!"

I was reminded how, two weeks earlier at Thanksgiving, I had only shared potential boy's names with our family.

Mark, always pragmatic, had suggested, "You know . . . we should probably have at least *one* girl name picked out, just in case."

"*Fine*," I had conceded. "We won't need it—but I'll choose one, just to make everyone happy."

And it's a good thing I did! Our beautiful daughter, Rachael Paulina Brisman, was born at 4:13 a.m. on December 6, 1996. She weighed eight pounds, seven ounces and was twenty-one inches long. Mark's tough exterior cracked, and he tearfully kissed me on the forehead and said, "You did good." He remained close as they placed our daughter near my face. I knew from the moment I saw her that it was right. She was the one we had been waiting for.

Maybe it was fate that I ended up having to stay in the hospital for an extra couple of days, as a massive blizzard had hit New York. When I was wheeled into a maternity room, my mother had the foresight to hang up a "Happy Channukah!" sign above my bedpost. I'd totally forgotten that the first night of Channukah had passed.

The excitement of being a new mom continued. Our parents and siblings visited us in the hospital as much as they could, armed with gifts for the raven-haired, strong infant. Jerry was particularly touched that we were able to arrange for Eva and him to come so he could meet his first granddaughter in person.

Meanwhile, my neuroticism and neediness caused bedlam in the hospital, especially when Mark went home. I couldn't seem to keep my finger off the buzzer to summon the nurse. Apparently, they had an unexpected baby boom that weekend, and the staff had a hard time keeping up. While Rachael took to nursing right away, I was unable to maneuver well with her in my hands and always seemed to require assistance to stand up and place her in the bassinet—especially with the morphine drip still in my arm. To my good fortune, the woman with whom I shared my room was already an experienced mom who joked that she would stay a week "to relax" if they'd let her. She was kind enough to press her own call button for me or dart into the hallway to fetch a nurse on my behalf.

Back in those days, paternity leave wasn't as much of a thing, and Mark returned to work while I was still in the hospital. I was all alone and caught off guard when a nurse entered, demanding to take Rachael "right now" for a private examination with the cardiologist.

A cardiologist! What?!

I burst into hysterics; I *did not* want them to take her, despite her assurances that that they'd tell me her status as soon as they knew anything. While I was still processing the shock of hearing this, she snatched the baby out my arms while I was trying to feed her and hurried off.

I called Mark at his office. I could hardly express myself through all the sobbing, but he got the general idea. "You know," Mark said, sounding very much like the lawyer husband, "She's *your* baby. If you don't want them to take her, you could just say *no*. You don't have to agree to anything. It's *your* decision."

I was reassured but also felt foolish I hadn't figured that out myself. I nearly tore my hair out during the hour I lay in bed, waiting. A female cardiologist casually appeared at the door with Rachael. In stark contrast to the way they had rushed her out of there, the doctor introduced herself and calmly started to relay what sounded like a medical school lecture. She described how the heart contains four chambers, blah-blah-blah...

I wish she'd get to the point already!

After a long-winded recitation, she finally informed me that Rachael had VSD (ventricular septal defect), a condition in which there is a tiny hole in one of the lower chambers of the heart. When the heart pumps blood, a little bit exits through that opening. They detected this at birth but hadn't said anything to Mark and me at the time. "It's fairly common," she explained. "About 10 percent of babies have it. Often, the situation rectifies itself and closes on its own over time—sometimes as soon as a week. It's something for us to watch, but nothing to get alarmed about."

Okay, sure, no cause for alarm: My baby has a hole in her heart!

After three days, the hospital discharged us without seeming the least bit concerned about the VSD issue. We scheduled a follow-up appointment with the cardiologist for a month later. I was terrified taking her home for the first time. How were we going to handle a fragile newborn baby with a heart issue?

Somehow, we managed to get her fastened in a car seat and headed off to our Bayside home. I could hardly wait to bring her into her new room that we had so thoughtfully prepared.

Upon entering our home, I was struck by one thing: The apartment was *freezing*. "Why is it so cold in here?!" I shouted at Mark.

"I left the windows opened a crack, just the way you like it," he answered.

"Right," I sheepishly said. I'd already forgotten how hot I had felt throughout my pregnancy and how my internal temperature must have been out of whack. "I'm not hot anymore and it's probably not good for the baby, so can you please close them?"

Mark dutifully raced around the apartment, slamming every window closed while I tried to get Rachael and myself situated.

The next few weeks were nerve-racking, to say the least. I'd rarely babysat when I was teenager—and never for an infant—so this was foreign to me. I still didn't feel well from the C-section, and Mark continued to commute to work in the city every day.

On several occasions, Rachael woke up screaming in the middle of the night. Apparently I'd diapered her incorrectly and her onesies were all wet. Bleary-eyed, I had to clean her off and start all over again with a fresh diaper and pajamas. Rachael didn't let me off the hook easily for my repeated blunders—and who can blame her?

Eventually, I got the hang of it—the breastfeeding, the diapering, the sleep schedule, and all the rest. Then again, it was difficult having a winter baby in New York, as it was too cold to take her out in the stroller, and we both needed fresh air. We also still had to contend with Rachael's heart issue. The follow-up visit with the cardiologist couldn't have come soon enough. After the examination, I learned that her heart was continuing to repair itself, although the defect was still detectable. The cardiologist gave me some minor instructions regarding limitations and care, and basically advised me not to worry about it. She wouldn't need a follow-up appointment for another four years. I called Mark from the car to tell him the good news.

Mark was an excellent father, a fact that didn't surprise me a bit. Although he worked a long day at his job, he was never too tired to interact with Rachael; in fact, it seemed to reenergize him. He changed his share of diapers, read board books such as *Goodnight Moon* to her, and spent many evenings lying on the couch with her sprawled fast asleep across his chest. He never minded when I thrust her in his arms as soon as he arrived home from work—usually when she was being fussy—and ordered, "Here you go, she's all yours!"

Mark hardly ever worked on Saturday or Sunday. He was a true "weekend daddy" and made every second count, wanting to spend as much time with Rachael as possible. Most nights though, we were content staying home and watching TV shows such as *Friends* and *Seinfeld*. "You are my lobster," he would turn to me and say, quoting an episode of *Friends* in which a character likens lobster couples to soulmates. I nicknamed Mark "Shmoopy," a joke I stole from a *Seinfeld* episode.

Rachael was an inquisitive and energetic baby, so there was little downtime, unless she was napping. She was a typical firstborn—super-confident and needy at the same time. She started saying words early and was walking with help between nine and ten months. "Carry you!" she'd shout at us, a term she learned after hearing us ask, "Would you like me to carry you?"

To help ensure she'd never feel alone, we bought a handy device called a Snap and Go. Her car seat fit inside it, which meant she could be wheeled from room-to-room, and it easily navigated the narrow halls and doorways of the apartment. She demanded that a parent always be visible to her at as soon as her eyes popped open. I was relieved to learn that other new parents were also at the mercy of their little tyrants, and I wasn't the only mom who had taken a shower with the curtain half open with the baby in close range.

Armonk, New York
May 1998–December 2000

We had begun to outgrow our space in Queens. After three and a half years of renting, Mark and I decided it was time to search for a permanent home. It seemed foolish to throw away money every month on something we would never own, and Mark was anxious for us to plant roots somewhere. We looked at parts of New Jersey where his coworkers lived and considered homes in new developments being built on Long Island—but nothing called out to us.

Westchester County, New York, was an entirely different matter. There were plenty of leafy, family-friendly towns to choose from, and its commutability to New York made it appealing.

After several weekends of touring neighborhoods and house hunting, we landed on a 2,800-square-foot, two-story contemporary home on a quarter of an acre plot in Armonk that had been built ten years prior. It was a long, rectangular-shaped home that had vertical gray wooden siding and was located within walking distance to town. Interestingly, it wasn't anything like what I had envisioned my dream home to look like. I had my heart set on something traditional and perhaps even antique. This house on Wampus Avenue seemed out of place amongst the others on the street, most of which were reminiscent of an earlier time and seemed to have more charm or character. When we first drove up to the house I told our real estate agent, "I don't think I want to go in."

Mark, ever the practical one who left emotion out of the decision, pointed out that this was a perfect starter house. It was situated in a great neighborhood that, with something of a stretch, we could afford. "All right, fine, I'll look," I conceded.

The inside belied the exterior. It was spacious and bright with a two-story entryway and a bright eat-in kitchen that adjoined the family room. The back of the kitchen featured sliding glass doors, which opened to a large deck than ran the length of the house. The large dining room/living room combo could easily accommodate a dozen people for the holiday dinners I envisioned. Meanwhile, the upstairs featured four nice-sized bedrooms and two full bathrooms. Everything felt new and immaculate; we wouldn't have to do any major renovation, which made it cost friendly.

The entire property was pancake flat (one of my wishes and probably a nod to my childhood on Long Island) and abutted acres of wetlands. The deceptively large backyard—which had a small wooden swing set already in place—sealed the deal. I could imagine children playing there.

We jumped on it right away. Its price tag—nearing $430,000—was at the highest end of our budget. We made a solid offer, and it was accepted. We took out a hefty mortgage, signed the papers, and moved in just in time to see the weeping cherry tree blossom in the front yard and delight in the full local suburban greenery. Mark and I couldn't have been more excited: our first house together. Our neighbors were everything we'd hoped for, friendly and welcoming; most had young children. The warm weather helped us get acquainted with everyone right away; all we had to do was walk out the front door and follow Rachael on her tricycle down the sidewalk. Backyard potluck dinners became the norm. It was also common to find neighborhood children running through the yard or even sneaking into my kitchen to peak into my fridge. Life was good.

Several years earlier, in 1995, Mark had happily put in his three years at the Bronx DA's office, sharpening his skills and gaining experience. He was equally as happy to leave it. He liked the job, but it was a dead end salary-wise, and he was hungry for new challenges. Every morning I would admire him in his suit before he'd head off to work with his big briefcase and cell phone, which was a novelty at that time. Sometimes I would be struck by how much he'd grown from that gangly, tall kid I'd met at that Long Island night club not that many years earlier.

Mark was ambitious, and a career in litigation continued to call to him. He was recruited as an associate attorney by the New York law firm of Lester Schwab Katz & Dwyer, LPP. Allan Fudim, one of the firm's partners, took Mark under his wing and mentored him. His career in litigation was officially underway as he worked toward partnership. He felt as if he'd finally made it to the big leagues. It was an excellent choice, and he hit the ground running. He was finally getting an opportunity to put all his years of practice and education to good use. The only downside was the hour-and-a-half commute. The firm was located on Broadway near Trinity Church, which meant a Metro-North train ride to Grand Central Station and then a subway downtown. The job ended up being demanding—as most legal jobs are—but Mark tried his best to arrive home by seven or seven thirty to enjoy a family dinner and spend some time with Rachael before she went to bed.

This became even more important with what was to come . . .

We had only lived in the house in Armonk for six months when I became pregnant with our second child. The morning sickness was even worse this time around. I tried to hide it from Rachael, but she was a keen observer and had recently turned two. "My mom's not feeling well," she'd matter-of-factly inform anyone in earshot, "She's sick."

Rachael relished the idea of having a sibling—so much so that we enrolled her in a class at the hospital where she and other tots could learn about babies and sibling etiquette. She seriously took this on and regularly practiced feeding and diapering one of her dolls.

Once again, Mark and I agreed we wanted to know the baby's gender. On this occasion, the technician and doctor believed the result to be conclusive: We were having a boy. I wanted to be elated, but settled on cautiously optimistic, as gender mistakes were not unheard of at that time.

We scheduled a C-section for August 13, 1999, with a new medical group affiliated with Northern Westchester Hospital (aka Mt. Kisco Hospital). We changed the date to August 16 once we realized the original appointment was Friday the thirteenth. We weren't the superstitious types, but then again, we weren't going to take any chances either.

This time around, Mark and I were a lot less stressed in the weeks leading up to the birth. We were old pros; we'd been through it all before. There was no doubt in our minds this would be simpler and easier since this wasn't going to be a natural delivery, and the timing wouldn't be in the baby's control.

We checked in, feeling confident and prepared compared to our first go-round nearly three years ago. Everything went as planned—inducement of labor, pain meds, prep for surgery—and we were good to go. Mark and I held hands. *Let's do this*!

It didn't take long for me to figure out something was amiss. I was feeling some things I hadn't experienced with Rachael. "Um . . . doctor?" I asked. "I don't think I'm numb. I'm having some sensations." After a few deliberate prods to my feet and other areas that I couldn't detect, the anesthesiologist declared that we were all clear and the surgery commenced.

Mark later confessed that he noticed the doctor eyeballing the anesthesiologist with concern. I shouldn't have been feeling *anything*. It wasn't exactly pain I was experiencing, and yet, the more they continued, the more I felt like a science experiment. There was noticeable moving, pulling, and shifting. I punctuated each sensation with an "oh!" or "ooh!" Mark later told me he had been looking on eagle-eyed, studying everything so he could recall it later, if need be.

My nerves eased when our son, William, entered this world at six in the morning on August 16 with similar dimensions as his sister: weighing eight pounds, eight ounces and measuring twenty-two inches long. As they placed him in my arms, I couldn't help but notice how perfect he seemed. His features were in beautiful balance, and he had wisps of light hair atop his head. The boy from my dreams had finally made his appearance.

The second time couldn't have been more different from the first. Aside from this being a summer birth, the entire hospital seemed empty. Not only did I have a single room, but most of the maternity wing was mine as well.

Physically, I felt far worse with this delivery. Something had obviously gone wrong with the anesthesia. Additionally, they gave me an oral pain reliever instead of the morphine drip, which was less effective. This didn't prevent the staff from forcing me to get on my feet as soon as possible. I wasn't yet up to having William rooming with me, so he spent much of the time in the nursery. During one stroll down the hall, I ventured to see my baby through the glass window. It struck me as odd that he was the only one in there.

"Where are all the other babies?" I asked the nurse.

"They're all in their rooms with their mothers," she answered.

I broke down in tears, unable to contain my guilt and shame. The nurse was quick to comfort me and had to walk me back to my room. "It's okay, it's all right. You're allowed to rest. You'll have plenty of time to spend with him."

The nurse eased my mind, which was a blessing because I wanted to be in good spirits for when Mark brought Rachael in for her first visit. I couldn't have been more excited to see her, but I was also concerned that she might unknowingly hurt me by getting too close. "Don't let her near the bed," I cautioned Mark over the phone.

When she bounced into the room, Mark scooped up William and sat down in a chair, Rachael following close behind. I'll never forget the enamored look on her face and the tender way she stroked him.

"I want to hold him," she squealed while crawling onto Mark's lap. They held him together. I looked on as he spoke gently to the pair. I tried not to get too emotional with tears of joy lest I manage to physically hurt myself in the process.

This is the perfect moment . . .

The following afternoon, I left the frigid air-conditioned hospital and faced the welcome August heat and sunlight. We buckled William into the car, and the three of us excitedly brought home the newest member of our family.

Our first order of business involved organizing William's bris, a Jewish circumcision ceremony that is required to take place eight days after a boy is born. This event is a celebratory event for the family and close relatives, who are subsequently invited to indulge in a feast of bagels, cream cheese, lox, and various high cholesterol/fatty Jewish foods. This would be our first major get-together in our house. Mark and I couldn't have been more thrilled that everything went off without a hitch. It marked the first time Jerry and Eva met my family.

Unfortunately, one week later, Roberta's health took a rapid turn for the worse. Lung cancer. It was a stressful, scary time for everyone—especially Mark. Thankfully, through successful treatments, Roberta was stabilized and able to resume most of her normal activities.

Soon after, things settled back into a routine, and I learned to juggle my life as a stay-at-home mom to two children. Needing the company and companionship of other adults while Mark put in long hours, I built a new community of friends in suburbia. Meanwhile, on the weekends, Mark did his best to be social while recovering from a week of grinding it out with his commute and long workdays. At times, we didn't see eye-to-eye regarding weekend activities. We compromised by prioritizing his family time while also giving me a respite from some domestic duties, like having a nice quiet dinner for the two of us or with friends.

I noticed that the pressure of trying to juggle it all was taking a toll on him. He was tempted to accept a position with a family law firm based in nearby White Plains. The stress would be greatly reduced, and he'd have much less commute time than with his current job. From my perspective, this sounded appealing because he'd finally have the work/life balance that he desperately wanted. But I didn't push him.

He viewed working for a small family firm as risky. He also believed the move could devastate his career. As he described, "I'd really like to be able to do this . . . but once you are out of being a New York City lawyer, you can't ever go back. And, if problems arise within the family or they run into financial troubles, I'm out of a job."

With the above in mind, he made the tough choice and declined the position. I supported him 100 percent.

The offer got Mark thinking, however, and he kept his options open. He knew he was young, smart, talented, and on the fast track for even greater things, so when another opportunity came knocking on the door, he had to look through the peephole and ask who was there.

Chapter Eleven

Office in the Clouds

Armonk, New York and New York, New York
January 1, 2001–September 3, 2001

From Mark's perspective, things couldn't be going better for him at Lester Schwab. He was making important connections, gaining firsthand experience, and heading along the partnership track. He enjoyed being a corporate defense attorney specializing in insurance defense cases. Among his clients was Hobart, which produced professional meat-slicing machines. When someone would receive an injury from using one of their products, Mark worked with his legal team to demonstrate that the manufacturer was not to blame for the unfortunate accident.

Best of all, he had a beloved coach and mentor, Allan Fudim, the senior partner who had brought Mark under his wing. A kind man with thick glasses and wavy hair parted in the middle, he treated Mark like a protégé, not a subordinate; they had mutual fondness for each other.

Toward the end of 2000, Mark started to get wind of some rumblings at the firm. He didn't tell me anything specific, only that there was some tension brewing among the partners. Mark didn't seem too concerned about it at the time, although it was difficult to tell if he knew more than he was letting on because he didn't want me to worry.

Everything changed one evening in January when Mark arrived home and said he had some important news to share with me.

"What? What is it?" I asked, always more anxious than my husband about matters that more directly impacted him.

"Allan told me he's leaving the firm," he reported.

"Really? Oh no," I gasped.

"It's not nearly as bad as it sounds, Jules," he said. "I received a very interesting offer."

"Okay," I absorbed, fearing the worst.

"I think I mentioned to you that Allan has poor eyesight?" Mark began.

"Yes, I remember."

"Well, unfortunately, his condition is chronic and deteriorating badly," he continued. "He told me that he's going to a firm called Harris Beach & Wilcox, where he's going to expand their presence in New York City and bring over a lot of his clients."

"What does this have to do with you?"

"He asked me to leave Lester Schwab and join him at his new firm. He says he can't work without me."

"Why would you follow him if your current role is secure?"

"This could be an even bigger opportunity. Allan trusts and confides in me. He wants me to be his 'eyes and ears.' He said, 'I know it's a leap of faith for you. But you'll be on an even faster track to partner. You'll inherit all my clients. There'll be a transition. I'll work for as long as I can. I promise I won't leave you hanging.'"

I could tell Mark was torn. This was not an easy decision. He was a loyal worker and fretted about the moral dilemma of leaving the company that had fostered him. On the other hand, he had to look out for his own interests, and there was no telling what he might be left with at his current firm without Allan there to have his back. Of course, there was also the lure of this grander opportunity that offered more money and a giant leap up the ladder. Mark also admired Allan and enjoyed working with him. It was telling to Mark that the lion's share of Allan's clients held him in such high esteem that they were following him to his next venture.

It took a few days for Mark to decide. Ultimately, he was swayed by something Allan had said to him: "The kingdom will be all yours." It was a major coup for Mark's career to be catapulted ahead like this at only thirty-three years of age. We both knew this was his true dream job.

Mark ended up being part of a larger company exodus, which caused ripples throughout the firm. Allan lured others away, including a valued employee named Pam—an administrative assistant with whom Mark was close.

As a result of the tumult, friendships were shattered. Carl, a young attorney who started working at the firm at roughly the same time as Mark, took his resignation personally; to say he felt betrayed and offended would be an understatement. "How could you do this to us?!" he assailed Mark, who was already wracked with guilt.

There was no fanfare when Allan, Mark, and the others headed out the door: no farewells, no parties, no thank-yous for their years of service. They expected such a reaction, I suppose, and were focused on what opportunities and challenges lay ahead. Allan's first order of business was planting the Harris Beach & Wilcox roots in downtown Manhattan and seeing what would grow.

A few years earlier, Mark and I could never have imagined he would find himself as high up in the clouds as Jack, the storybook character who climbed the legendary beanstalk.

Two World Trade Center, otherwise known as the South Tower, was completed in 1973. At the time, it was the second tallest building in the world (1,362 feet to the roof). Only its twin, One World Trade Center, stood higher (by a narrow six feet), although the former had more floors (110). Situated not far from Wall Street, the Towers had their own zip code (10048) and subway station (WTC Cortland Station). By 2001, nearly one hundred businesses rented space in the South Tower; that year, one of its newer tenants—the law firm of Harris Beach & Wilcox—settled into the eighty-fifth floor and commenced major renovations.

Although I never discouraged Mark from working at Two World Trade Center, I did openly share my reservations about being on such a high floor in a gargantuan building. He always laughed off my acrophobia, calling me an alarmist and adding, "You know, there are floors even higher than mine."

He had a few goals in mind when he invited me to visit his office: ease my concerns about the building, impress me with his new digs, and show off his wife to his colleagues. I didn't mind his last two motivations, but I had doubts about him being able to convince me about the first one.

I had a bad feeling about going to the building from the start but realized I couldn't say no to his request. At some point, I knew I'd have to summon my courage and take Metro North into Grand Central, followed by the 1 Train to WTC Cortland Station.

Right away, I despised the World Trade Center's height and elevator ride, which made a strange humming noise on the way up and caused my ears to pop.

This place is just too high . . . it feels like a bird's nest in the sky.

I pulled myself together and plastered a smile on my face as the elevator doors opened on the eighty-fifth floor. I was subsequently buzzed into the Harris Beach & Wilcox waiting area. Mark raced out to greet me before I had a chance to sit down on the leather couch. He excitedly gave me a tour around the office. The professional office struck me as new and immaculate to the point of feeling sterile. Glass seemed to shine at me from all directions. It felt modern and high tech, although it wasn't as if I'd seen many other professional offices at that time. There was plenty of new construction still in the works and some furniture still on the way in what I'd heard was an ongoing $4 million renovation project.

Mark seemed comfortable and in his element in this space, although he hadn't been in it for long. He called out to introduce me to the team, which formed something of a welcome wagon. They were all warm and friendly, saying things such as "Mark talks about you all the time." Pam made an especially grand gesture, greeting me with a powerful hug.

He brought me into his spacious office with glass windows that offered a beautiful view of Manhattan, which I refused to look through. His office was spotless and organized in much the way I expected it to be. On his mahogany desk, he had a desktop computer, legal pad, fine pen, and framed photos of us from our wedding—as well as those of Rachael and William—but that was it. The walls were neatly adorned with his Bar Association documentation and diplomas.

It felt good to see that Mark was proud to display our relationship, especially since his work world seemed so distant from our family life. I had deep admiration for his accomplishments and the fact that he'd "made it." He was happy here. He *belonged* here.

Mark's commute and work hours were roughly the same as in his last position. He left for the train early in the morning and typically didn't return home until seven thirty at night, after which much of the main activities with the kids had already occurred. Often I was focused on wrangling them to go to sleep, and Mark would be hungry and exhausted, but never complained about his long day or work problems. He continued to have a gift for compartmentalizing work and keeping it separate from our private universe in Armonk. At the same time, his old-school stodginess amused me. He liked wearing his suit and tie every day and bristled when the company implemented dress-down Fridays. He believed a law firm should always maintain its professional image and that people would slack off if they weren't wearing proper attire. It took some getting used to for him to leave for work in collared shirt and slacks on these more casual days.

As if his schedule wasn't busy enough, Mark occasionally volunteered on weekdays to serve as a guest speaker at his alma mater, NYU School of Law. He would join in on what they referred to as "Moot Court" for classes, simulating the courtroom experience. He would help instruct and/or create mock scenarios for students on how to present cases for litigation and choose jurors. It became something of a passion for him to give back to his alma mater and help groom young attorneys.

Meanwhile, I managed most things at home with the kids. I had plenty to do keeping the house in order and busied myself shepherding the kids to and from preschool or playdates. During my free time, I socialized with other local moms who also spent much of their weekdays solo. Despite this and the fact that Mark was always around and attentive on weekends, I experienced periods of loneliness. I thought he might be able to catch a break and loosen up his schedule in the summer, but he was unable to pull this off as he was still too new in the company, and the New York office was just getting off the ground. We also didn't have enough money or free time to go on a real vacation together—with or without the kids. There were some days I regretted he hadn't taken the simpler job in White Plains so he could have been more available to us.

We did find ways to maximize the last hurrah of the summer: Labor Day weekend. My parents, along with my friend Alison and her family, joined all four of us for a spectacular day at Adventureland amusement park in East Farmingdale. The sun could not have shone brighter. Mark became a kid again, taking every opportunity to accompany the kids on all the rides—sometimes multiple times. It was hilarious seeing his elongated frame stuffed into the kiddie airplane with Rachael. We enjoyed the usual amusement park fare—hot dogs, ice cream, and so on—and snapped as many photographs as we could. It was probably the most fun we ever had together as a family, and I was so happy my parents and friends were able to share the day with us.

We spent the Monday of Labor Day weekend in the backyard of local friends, where all the kids ran under a sprinkler, dove across a Slip 'N Slide, splashed in a kiddie pool, dug shovels into a sandbox, and otherwise giddily ran around, laughing and screaming with delight. While I chatted with the moms, Mark sat back in a lawn chair, drank beer, and became better acquainted with the dads.

That didn't prevent him from conducting some community business. Once the neighbors realized they had a Manhattan attorney in their midst, they set their sights on recruiting him to do something about the crazy drivers kamikazeing through our street. This became especially problematic when there were so many cars in the vicinity for practices and games at the nearby soccer field. A child was bound to get hurt crossing the street. The parents had attempted to get something done—suggesting a stop sign, speed bumps, etc.—to no avail.

As it happened, there was enough noise made about the problem that we were granted an audience with the superintendent of schools on September 12. Mark already began scribbling notes on a legal pad in preparation for this meeting. At home, he added a reminder about the event in bold marker to our wall calendar.

Mark was a man of his word, and everyone counted on him being present for that town meeting. Due to circumstances well beyond his—or anyone's control—this was not to be.

Chapter Twelve

Missing Persons

Armonk, New York and New York, New York
September 4, 2001–September 11, 2001

The great summery weather continued the entire week following Labor Day. Our kids weren't starting school until Monday, September 10, so I had a few extra days keeping them busy at the playground at the end of the street, riding their respective bikes, or perhaps motoring down the sidewalk in Rachael's pink electric car—a gift from the grandparents.

The vibe in the house was one of excitement because William was on the verge of starting preschool at the Rosenthal Jewish Community Center in Pleasantville. For Mark and me, it felt like something of an accomplishment to have endured the toddler years and reached the milestone of both children in school. I was particularly overjoyed by the prospect of having some free time to myself—even if only for several hours—without the kids around 24-7.

The week progressed with a few interesting developments. Mark was scheduled to go on a rare business trip out of town that week to meet with a client, so Jill, my sister, arranged to drive from her home in Sharon, Massachusetts, on Monday to spend a few days in Armonk to keep me company. Jill and her husband, David (who remained in Massachusetts), now had a boy, Joseph (nicknamed Little Joe), who was about the same age as William (nicknamed Boodles), and we thought it would be a great opportunity for them to play together. As icing on the cake, my parents planned to drive to my house on Tuesday to visit their two daughters' families at the same time.

Over the weekend, however, Mark received a call from Allan. For whatever reason—perhaps the client specified he wanted the boss instead of an associate—Allan was going to take his place for the upcoming business trip. Mark wasn't disappointed at all; if anything, he was pleased with the change in plans, preferring to work in the office. A man who genuinely enjoyed his daily routine, Mark disliked traveling and being away from home. And now he could play host to his sister-in-law and nephew, something he enjoyed doing.

That Monday evening, Mark uncharacteristically arrived home early from the city, probably so he could spend more time with our guests. As he stepped in the door, he slapped his hands together and, in a cheerful voice asked, "What's for dinner?"

Realizing I was short on a few kitchen supplies, I asked Jill and Mark if it would be all right if I made a quick run to the supermarket. They waved me off, saying they had the house and kids under control.

Jill later told me that while I was out, Mark gave her and his nephew his full attention, setting up the guest room and serving snacks and drinks. When he asked her if she needed anything else, she answered, "Now that you mention it, I sort of forgot my toothbrush..."

He snapped his fingers and blurted, "No problem!"

A few moments later, he reappeared carrying a brand-new toothbrush still in its plastic casing. Mark, always prepared, kept spares of pretty much everything for times like these. "I have plenty of toothpaste if you need it . . . floss, too!"

"No, thanks, we're good," she chuckled.

As soon as I returned home, I rushed to the kitchen with the shopping bags to start dinner. I figured I'd make one of my specialties—spaghetti with homemade meat sauce—as I knew it was something Mark loved and the kids would appreciate. Jill assisted with setting the table and getting the kids washed up.

The two of us reveled in the moment: We were two sisters, now moms with sons the same age. We lived several hours apart and had a lot to catch up on.

At some point, Jill turned the subject to Mark. "He seems so happy here," she observed.

"Yeah, he has so little time with us during the week," I said, adding, "He makes it count."

"Yes. I also mean that it seems like he's creating the life he's always wanted," she explained. "He's got his little family and a nice home in an ideal setting. Sort of like he's living in a Norman Rockwell painting."

"I think it's great," Jill emphasized.

I agreed with her, realizing this is how it seemed to someone on the outside looking in. I imagined if Mark had been asked if he wanted anything else in life he would have cited only one thing—becoming a partner in the firm—which was already well within his grasp. I doubted he wanted or needed anything else—except maybe a family dog, which we were not quite ready for yet.

We had a wonderful dinner, after which Mark helped clean up. We made sure to get our kids into bed early, so they would be fresh for school the next morning. Mark and I said goodnight to Jill and the kids, and retired to our bedroom for the remainder of the evening.

We cuddled and made light conversation about the following day and the kids' preschool arrangements. It was understood that

Mark intended to take his early morning train while I would shepherd William and Rachael to school. I told Mark I looked forward to spending the day with Jill and Little Joe, as well as my parents, who were arriving later that day.

"Tomorrow's a big day for William," Mark said with pride, but I could hear the tiredness in his voice. "The first drop off without the parents hovering about. I expect he'll do fine but please fill me in on all the details."

"Okay," I acknowledged. "And try to take the earlier train home again, if you can."

We fell asleep in each other's arms. All remained quiet and peaceful. It was just another Monday evening in the Brisman home in Armonk, New York. Tomorrow was Tuesday September 11, 2001—a date that didn't seem to have any special significance in my family's life.

Until it did.

I rarely heard Mark's movements around the bedroom as he readied himself in the early mornings but, for some reason, I was awake in bed on this particular day. His routine was the same as always, and he hardly made a sound; even so, I was restless and couldn't stop tossing and turning. I rolled over and tried to go back to sleep, not saying a word.

I was vaguely aware of when he left the bedroom and popped into William's room. I imagined him kissing him on the forehead and saying something like, "Good luck at school, Boodles." I'm sure he peeked in on Rachael, too, his princess.

Then, as usual, he headed off with his briefcase to the station to catch his train.

About forty-five minutes later, I woke up, showered, got

dressed, helped William and Rachael prepare for school, and ate a quick breakfast with them, Jill, and Joseph. At about eight thirty, I ushered my kids into the car and drove off to the school on what was yet another beautiful sunny day.

I pulled into the school parking lot and maneuvered the kids out of the car. On entering the building, I led the kids to their respective classrooms. Rachael, familiar with the drill, ran right in yelling, "Bye, Mommy!" without looking back.

William stepped into his classroom with both purpose, where he was greeted by his three teachers. I hovered in the doorway, waiting for him to grant me permission to leave.

On my out, I heard some parents chattering in the hallway. I stopped short when someone casually said, "The World Trade Center Tower One was just hit."

"I think it was a bomb," someone else added.

I became numb. Mark worked in Tower Two, but this was way too close for comfort. I felt around in my bag for my phone, but it wasn't there. I hurried out of the school and ran across the parking lot toward my car. I was relieved to see my phone in the driver's seat. Sure enough, I had missed a call while I was inside . . . from Mark. Unfortunately, he hadn't left a message. I dialed his cell phone number, which went straight to voice mail. I called his office, where there was no answer. I redialed both repeatedly as I raced back to the house.

I burst through the front door, where I was immediately met by my sister. "Jill, something happened at Tower One of the World Trade Center—a bomb or something. Did Mark call?"

"Yes," she answered in a calm voice. "I spoke to him. He said he's okay and he's coming home."

"Thank God," I sighed.

I continued hitting auto dial of Mark's number as we moved toward the family room, where the television had already been turned on. The network's regular programming had been interrupted by the breaking news: at 8:46 a.m., American Airlines Flight 11 had flown straight into Tower One of the World Trade Center. It was surreal watching the news footage.

How is this possible? Where is the news about all those people inside and nearby? They aren't saying anything about Tower Two . . .

Seventeen minutes later, at 9:03, a *second* plane—United Airlines Flight 175—careened into Tower Two of the World Trade Center. Mark, my husband—the love of my life—worked there, on the eighty-fifth floor. I prayed he had been doing what he told Jill: heading straight home. But would he? *Did* he?

My fingers could not move fast enough as I repeatedly dialed Mark's number.

Voice mail. Again. Again. And again.

I stared at the phone in utter desperation.

Why isn't he answering his phone? Mark would NEVER leave me hanging like this. If there were a way to reach me, he would do it. Maybe the cell phones are out of service?

I barely caught the television reportage as more events unfolded. At 9:37, a third plane, American Flight 175, descended into the west side of the US Pentagon. But this was still far from the end of it. At 10:03, a fourth plane—United Airlines Flight 93 heading for a government building target in Washington, D.C.—fell from the sky and landed in a field near Shanksville in Sommerset County, Pennsylvania. Back in New York, at 9:59, Tower Two collapsed, followed by Tower One just less than a half an hour later.

I struggled to keep up as more information began to emerge: Four airplanes had been simultaneously hijacked by terrorists—later confirmed as al-Qaeda—with the intent of demolishing symbols of American Democracy and capitalism. The terrorist plot had all been meticulously planned well in advance to inflict as much damage, loss, pain, and suffering on American life as possible. It was assumed there were no survivors aboard any of the airplanes. No one seemed to know much about what had been happening on the ground just yet, except that brave New York firefighters and police officers had swarmed inside the World Trade Center buildings with lightning speed to evacuate as many people as possible. At this point, it was unknown how many—*if* any—people might have managed to escape the collapse. I continued to hold out hope for Mark's survival.

He said he was "going home," right? Maybe he got out of there before the airplane hit his building . . .

My land line and cell phone were barraged by calls: friends, family members, neighbors . . . and then by Mark's colleagues, who either hadn't gone into the office at all that day or had gone in later and been turned away or those who went down the eighty-five flights of stairs to safety when they heard about what had happened to Tower One. I was also informed of a few who had made it down in the elevators, which sounded encouraging. The news also showed masses of people walking on foot across the Brooklyn Bridge, as traffic and public transportation had ground to a dead stop. I was hopeful Mark was one of those confused and dazed people making their way out—most of whom were without their belongings or any means to tell their loved ones they were okay.

Allan, who had heard about events while traveling in Mark's place, was among those who called. He sounded shaken up but tried to remain upbeat and optimistic. "Have you heard from Mark?" he demanded.

When I told him I hadn't, he added, "Others in the office are being accounted for, Juliette. I'm sure he's all right—Mark's a smart guy, he made his way out. Could you let me know as soon as you hear anything?"

I was thankful for two things: My kids were at school and Jill was with me. I don't know what I would have done had I been alone or responsible for children during this terrifying time.

I leapt up each time any phone rang. One call, from someone who worked in Mark's office, kindled some hope. "Mark is confirmed," he said before hanging up.

Confirmed? Does that mean confirmed alive or confirmed dead?

Jill and I took it to mean the former; he'd been spotted and had escaped the building in time.

But . . . if that's true . . . why hasn't he called me? Even if he's hurt, hospitalized, or helping others, he would stop everything to let me know he was safe. Maybe he lost his phone, or it was damaged in all the ruckus? Maybe he decided to do the long walk across the bridge instead of taking the train home?

We flipped TV channels to see if any station had anything new to share. All we saw were the same images of the planes flying into buildings. The same masses of concrete, metal, rubble, and dust piling down from the sky. Over and over and over . . . then we saw a fireball of a man spiral down the exterior of the building amidst the smoke.

My parents arrived at the house. They hadn't been listening to the radio in the car, so they had no idea of what had happened. Jill and I filled them in as best as we could without breaking down. They joined us in the family room and immediately became transfixed by the television reporting. When it was time for me to pick up the kids from preschool, I took them along. Fortunately, Rachael and William were so happy to see them and then distracted by the other family members when we arrived home, that I was able to concentrate on other matters.

The phone calls were incessant, hour after hour. More family, friends, and people from Mark's office. They pitched in and contacted every hospital in Manhattan, Brooklyn, and Queens for any sign of him. Neighbors who had heard the news and were aware that Mark worked at the World Trade Center stopped by to add their prayers and support. Mark's siblings dropped whatever they were doing and made beelines to our house. Everyone was panic-stricken and devastated.

It was five p.m. Not a peep from Mark. By this time, my thoughts had turned to the darkest, worst-case scenario. Despite the earlier confirmation, I didn't think Mark had made it out. He would have called me, hell or highwater. That caller had given me misinformation and false hope.

The sun went down on the evening of 9/11/2001. Reality set in. I stopped watching TV.

Mark isn't ever coming home. It's just me now. My children have lost their father.

I felt ill, nonfunctioning. My brain and body separated. Jill and Michelle had to help me upstairs to my room and onto my bed. I curled under the covers and asked out loud, "Why is this happening?"

A little while later, Michelle brought up something on a tray for me to eat. I don't recall what it was, but I couldn't find a way to consume it. Instead, I drank a box of Parmalat chocolate milk, as it was the only substance I was able to choke down.

I became so overwrought and afraid to be alone that my mother had to sleep next to me. It was a miracle my parents happened to be visiting that day and had left their house early enough to cross the bridges before they were closed for safety reasons. I could not have survived this without their support.

I broke down and cried in the middle of the night and continued straight into the early morning. I did this alone in my bathroom to avoid attracting attention. Part of me thought it was better to get it all out, by myself, instead of in front of the kids. I didn't want them to see or hear me in this state, so I closed the door and ran water in the sink to muffle the sounds of my sobs. The tears flowed freely. Eyeing my reflection in the mirror probably didn't help matters, but I didn't want to sit in darkness, either.

I was surprised when my emotional upheaval came to an abrupt halt, but I welcomed it. My body stopped convulsing with tears and a feeling of calm and stillness took its place. I soaked it in. After a brief period, I felt relaxed and exhausted enough to return to bed, where I fell into a deep sleep for a few hours.

September 12: The frenzy continued. The phone calls and neighbor visits resumed. People continued to contact Manhattan area hospitals to see if by some miracle an unidentified patient who fit Mark's description had materialized there. This was prior to the public learning that there were virtually no patients admitted anywhere. Everyone asked the same question, "Have you heard *anything*?," and tried to be hopeful. But I knew it was hopeless.

My parents, who had slept over, went home to pick up a few things and then returned. David, Jill's husband, drove from their home in Massachusetts to be with us.

Some close family couldn't make it to my house right away, even though they wanted to be there. Mark's siblings provided comfort to Roberta in Bayside. I commiserated by phone with Jerry and Eva in Pennsylvania, who informed me they were making plans to drive to Armonk.

All I could think about was how I was going to convey the tragic news to William and Rachael. I knew this was going to be a tremendous challenge. They were so young, and I was afraid that a misstep could cause permanent psychological damage. I decided I had to hold off saying anything until I had solid direction on how to best handle it. Instead, for the time being I said to them, "Don't worry. Your daddy is away on a business trip. He will be away for a while..."

The total number of lives claimed on 9/11 is calculated at 2,977. Of these, 2,753 were killed at the World Trade Center. An additional 6,000 people were injured. None of this can begin to factor in the long-term effects the toxic smoke inhalation had upon all the civilians, rescuers, medical personnel, volunteers, and residents in the vicinity, nor can it begin to consider the mental and emotional health of survivors, witnesses, and their families—mine included.

While the numbers represent the worst terrorist attack on American soil in our history and cannot be understated, the toll would have been far worse if the attacks had occurred a bit later in the day. There were many people who arrived at the World Trade Center after the first or second strike and were turned away by police and firefighters.

Over time, I learned the painful details of what likely unfolded on the eighty-fifth floor of the South Tower on the morning of 9/11. While I recognize I will never know anything with 100 percent certainty, the eyewitness accounts survivors provided to Square One Investigations (a private investigation firm) are as close as I will ever get to finding out what happened in Mark's final hours. One thing is clear: The fate of individuals' lives was determined based on where they were at the time, what they were doing, and the split-second decisions they made.

Among the one hundred workers employed by Harris Beach & Wilcox in this location (including Bowne Business Solutions personnel, a firm that provided mailroom/office services), under twenty were present in the office that morning (excluding several construction workers). Mark, who was known as among the first to arrive in the office, was spotted as having been present.

When Tower One was hit, a construction worker advised a receptionist named Phyllis Tackel to evacuate, which she did. Terry

Mikell, a secretary, saw the black smoke and debris out the window and was informed by another secretary, Anne Pampinella, that a "construction accident" at Tower One had been the cause of the problem. Anne, along with attorneys Julissa Gomez and Andrew Zucker, went around the office directing people to leave. The land phone lines stopped functioning, which means it was probably somewhere around this time that Mark tried and failed to reach me by cell phone but then spoke to Jill at my house.

At first, several people didn't take the situation seriously; Mark was among them. Julissa later recounted that she called out to Mark to exit, but he didn't appear to be in any kind of hurry to move. Knowing Mark as I do, I can imagine him being unfazed—calm, cool, and collected—and thinking this was going to turn out to be much ado about nothing. I can visualize him taking his time to finish typing a sentence on a legal brief and then scanning his office for essentials to stuff in his briefcase. PA announcements advising people to shelter in place for safety reasons probably convinced him there was nothing to worry about; that this was all just a nuisance to put a wrench in his day.

While thousands of workers descended the stairs in an organized fashion and others waited to cram into elevators, a massive impact rocked the building. In the stairwells, the floors buckled, the walls cracked, and plaster fell.

Andrew Zucker, who had initially exited with Anne Pampinella, turned back to the office to compel Mark and another attorney, Joanne Weil, to leave. It seems as if Mr. Zucker caught up with them because Mark was seen heading out of the office with his briefcase. Office Manager Cynthia Hauer, who had made it to the stairs, recalled that Mr. Zucker, Ms. Weil, and Mark were trailing behind her, but was uncertain of whether they were heading toward the stairs or to the elevator.

It remains unknown whether something happened to Mark

as he waited by the elevator or, if he made it inside one, it failed to reach its destination on the ground floor for obvious reasons. Another possibility is that he may have been impatient waiting for the elevator—or suddenly deemed it unsafe—and changed his escape plan to the stairs (but too late). Or . . . he may have been waiting by the elevator, heard and felt the explosion of the airplane hitting the building, and then raced to the stairwell (too late).

Whatever the case, as the day progressed, Mark was identified as among the six "missing and unaccounted for" persons from the eighty-fifth floor. The other individuals were attorneys Weil and Zucker, staff members Irina Kolpakova and Sharon Millan, and construction manager Hector Tamayo. All the other previously named workers made it out alive before Tower Two caved.

I can't even imagine what Mark and the others who were lost endured during their final moments. I feel deep admiration for Mr. Zucker, who gave his life to go back to try and save Mark and the others. I hope and pray that it happened so rapidly they didn't know what hit them and didn't feel a split second of pain or suffering. There is the belief in Judaism that the soul doesn't depart from the physical world right away; it needs time to acclimate and adjust to death. The belief is also that the soul is not alone during this process but mirrors our experience as mourners.

I'd like to believe Mark's "presence" helped soothe me in my time of need. Hopefully, being close to me in whatever way was possible was comforting to him, too.

To all who were tragically lost that day:

yehi zichra baruch
May their memory be a blessing

Chapter Thirteen

Picking up the Pieces

Armonk, New York
September 12, 2001–September 2002

I found out right away there isn't a playbook on the right way to think or behave when something so inexplicable and of such tragic magnitude occurs. Only a day earlier, I was one half of a strong team; the next day merely one half. The day before, my children had two parents; today, only one. What is a mother—a new *widow*, if I could ever get accustomed to that word—to do to resume any kind of normalcy? What is the right way for her to explain this to her kids?

As crazy as this might sound, I drove Rachael and William to preschool as usual on Wednesday, September 12. Why? Several reasons, starting with ensuring that they would endure as little pain as possible and not suffer from lingering, preventable scars years later. I needed everything to be in order with them. Telling them about their father had to be handled right—and I didn't have a clue what that meant yet.

At the same time, my main priority was figuring out how I would somehow get through this. I knew if I couldn't function, the kids would surely be affected. For my own health and sanity, I had to have a clear head and a few free hours during the day to focus, get things done, and release my emotions without my children seeing me break down.

During the drop-off at school, I was met with the stunned gazes of parents and teachers. Word had already spread about Mark's presumed fate on 9/11, and I was the last person they expected to see at school. They weren't being judgmental; they just couldn't believe I would be visible so soon and bring my kids there the day after such a loss. Most other parents didn't know what to make of this or what to say to me—some embraced me silently while others made certain to avoid eye contact. The teachers were professional and gracious, however, offering to do whatever was necessary to help, which included keeping Rachael and William for extra time after school, if I required such assistance.

Meanwhile, people continued to reach out, email, and even show up at my front door with food. From their collective grief was born a desire to do something and contribute in some way. I was deeply moved by this outpouring of support, but conflicted, too, as dealing with all this attention required a substantial amount of energy. Amidst all this outpouring of concern came the realization that I might be the subject of pity—a possibility I tried not to think about—and made me feel panicked and anxious, as it somehow confirmed a hopelessness about my current situation.

There was one connection from outside my immediate circle who was timely and made a major difference: a fellow preschool mom named Bonnie. She managed to get my number and say to me, "Juliette, if you need anything at all, I can help you through it. I'm a social worker by training."

I didn't hesitate and asked to meet with her in person as soon as possible. She appeared at my house in what seemed like less than an hour. I barely knew Bonnie, but, in my desperation for guidance,

I let down my guard and tearfully bombarded her with questions. I immediately determined she could help, as her style was a good balance of empathy and no-nonsense problem solving. My mind was racing to find answers to the following:

What should I say?
What should I not say?
When is the right time?
Where should this happen and with whom?
Should the kids go to the cemetery, the memorial service, and other events that arise?

It became plain from our conversation that Rachael had to be told sooner, rather than later. She was a sharp and precocious almost five-year-old who had been extremely close to her father. I knew I could not put telling her off much longer.

William, who had turned two the previous month, didn't require much of a strategy. This was a relief on the one hand, but incredibly heartbreaking on the other. Bonnie advised that, at his stage of development, the loss would be far less distressing and possible signs of grief more subtle. If William continued to feel cared for and secure, he should adjust reasonably well to "the new normal."

Over the next few days, Bonnie and I created a game plan with a written script. The goal was to be truthful, straightforward, and age appropriate, while divulging as little as possible to avoid causing unnecessary upset. I tried to anticipate what questions Rachael might ask and had prepared answers at the ready.

The following Saturday, September 16, I assembled our closest family members—grandparents, aunts, uncles, and cousins—at our house with the message: "I would like you to be present when we tell Rachael. It will be a shock for her, but my hope is it will ease the blow to see all the people she has in her life who love her."

The original intent was for me to speak with Rachael alone in my bedroom, as it seemed to be the most comforting place for her. While I recited words from the script, the assembled family members would wait for us to come into the family room downstairs, at which point they would demonstrate their love and support for her.

When the time came, however, I must have seemed shaky enough for Jill, Michelle, and Jaci to join me as we headed upstairs toward my bedroom with Rachael and sat on the bed. I took my daughter's hands and looked her in the eyes as I nervously began, "There is something I need to tell you about Daddy."

Rachael seemed to sense something was up right from the beginning. She focused all her attention on me as I took a deep breath and said, "Something happened to Daddy while he was at work. There was an ..."

My pause between words must have seemed like I was stumbling, so Michelle jumped in with the words "... an accident at his building" to complete my sentence.

"Yes," I continued. "A lot of people got hurt and died. Daddy ... your father ... also ..."

Michelle once again came to the rescue while I choked on the words. I didn't mind a bit. "Your daddy was one of the people who died in the building."

Tears filled Rachael's eyes, although she may have been doing so because she thought it was expected of her. The adults allowed the words to linger in the air for a moment.

"You can ask any questions you like, Rachael," I offered.

"He's ... *dead*? Really? Are you *sure*?" she processed.

"Yes, we're sure," I answered.

"Does that mean I can't play 'gym daddy' with him anymore?"

"That's right," I confirmed, holding in my own tears and stroking her hair. "He won't be coming home. I'm so sorry."

"But ... he was my favorite one in the house."

It didn't bother me that I had been second fiddle to Mark. She had always been a daddy's girl. "I know," I mustered.

"I have no daddy," she stated, almost matter-of-factly. "I have nobody else but you."

I could not respond.

"He's still your daddy," Michelle intervened. "He will *always* be your daddy. He's in heaven."

Rachael considered that statement for a few moments.

Our messaging seemed good enough, at least for the time being. A child can only stay put for so long, so I wasn't surprised when she announced, "I want to play with my cousins."

"Okay," I said. "Let's go downstairs and see our family. Everyone who loves you is here. Then you can play with your cousins."

I exchanged glances with the three women. They nodded to indicate we'd accomplished the task as well as it could have been done. And at least I had one less heavy burden to carry on my slanted shoulders.

There were seemingly endless things to do and decisions to make—none of which I was prepared for. I had to produce Mark's DNA for the New York Police Department's ongoing investigations as remains were found and processed. I also answered several calls from them about what he had been wearing and what might have been on him that day. Although I hadn't watched him dress that morning, I had no doubt he was wearing his usual suit, tie, white-collared shirt, dress shoes, etc.—as if any of that would have mattered at that point. They were well past the point of searching for living people; now it was all about recovery and identification before all of Ground Zero—as the World Trade Center area became known—was cleared away.

Whenever I spoke to a detective—a different one each time—I reported the same details about what items I thought were on my husband: an intricately designed gold mezuzah on a chain he'd received at his Bar Mitzvah and never removed, his black-banded watch, his soft leather briefcase, his wallet and car keys, and his plain gold wedding band matching mine with hammered edges and no inscription.

Next came one of the most difficult decisions of all: How to best honor Mark? Should we arrange an ad hoc funeral at a cemetery? Should there first be a memorial service? Or maybe we should do both—or neither?

There are plenty of rules and customs in Judaism regarding how remembrances, funeral services, and sitting shiva should be handled. In the Jewish faith, shiva is the seven-day period of formal mourning for the dead and begins immediately after the funeral. During this time, mourners—which includes spouses, parents, siblings, and adult children—are prohibited from, among other things, looking at their reflections in mirrors (which is why they are covered, usually with sheets), working, and listening to music.

I was dismayed to learn that our 5,800-year-old religion that covered death-related behavior and rituals with such specificity did not provide instruction for circumstances when the individual is missing but presumed lost without any remains. There are no protocols for these situations. We would have to wing it, which may have been even more difficult, for now there were choices to be made—not to mention people's feelings and preferences to consider.

Complicating matters was the fact that Mark and I hadn't yet settled on a neighborhood synagogue. We had some conversations and visited a few but didn't see any sense of urgency to join one, since our kids were too young. We figured we'd become members of a congregation once we registered Rachael for Hebrew school.

The synagogue matter ended up being settled for me when

Rabbi Douglas Krantz of Congregation B'Nai Yisrael in Armonk reached out to me—the only area clergy member to do so. He struck me as a kind, sympathetic man, and he didn't pressure me about anything. "There are no rules," he alerted me. "You can do whatever it is you want to do. Do what you feel is right for Mark's memory and for you and your immediate family." He offered his services and use of the temple for our needs without any obligation.

Some decisions were no-brainers. I didn't want to place Mark's picture on the fence of Trinity Church with other MIA 9/11 people; I didn't see any point in it. I didn't attend or watch any of the 9/11 concerts (such as the one with Paul McCartney). I had no interest in visiting Ground Zero or even venturing into the city. Thankfully, I wasn't sought out by the press, since at the time I didn't want to give interviews or have any kind of spotlight shined on me. I became fearful and vulnerable without Mark by my side. One of my main goals was to stay as safe and protected as possible and mourn in my own way and in my own time—*privately*.

With Rabbi Krantz's guidance and support—as well as input from Mark's family—I managed to think through how I wanted to honor Mark. We arranged for a memorial service on September 23 at Congregation B'Nai Yisrael with multiple speakers—including myself—followed by a traditional cemetery burial. After much deliberation, I decided to bring Rachael and William to both events, despite recommendations to the contrary from some family members who thought it might be too upsetting to them or me. Ultimately, it was Bonnie who helped me make the call. "You absolutely need to bring them," she insisted.

"Why?" I asked.

"Later on, whey they are older, they are going to ask you if they went to the service. You want to be able to tell them yes. Even if they don't remember it, it's important that you can truthfully say yes to them, so they feel like they were part of it," she explained.

I thought her rationale made complete sense and went with it. Both children were too young to fully comprehend what was happening anyway and too restless to sit still through such a lengthy service. I would leave it up to them if they preferred to leave the sanctuary to explore one of the classrooms under the watchful eye of a relative.

The September 23 memorial service was open to anyone who wished to attend. I expected a large turnout but nothing like what ended up happening. The sanctuary was jam-packed with wall-to-wall people, some of whom had traveled far and wide: friends (from Mark's childhood to present), family, coworkers, congregants, neighbors, clergy (including Cantor Tyrone Bauer, the rabbi who Bar Mitzvahed Mark and his siblings, and married us nearly eight years earlier), and complete strangers of all religions and persuasions who felt the need to be a part of this—perhaps to commiserate or to come to terms with 9/11. It became clear to me that the wounds of that day cut deep into the hearts of all Americans—not just to those close to the ones who were lost. The whole country was still in deep mourning.

That day, I wore a simple black two-piece suit (without any kind of hat or veil) from my closet that billowed off me. I'd lost a lot of weight in the two weeks following 9/11 because I had no appetite. My main sustenance during this period were those boxes of Parmalat chocolate milk, the liquid always somehow managed to slide down my throat and into my stomach.

I composed myself for that day by going on what I can only describe as emotional autopilot. Some people may have interpreted my expressions and calm demeanor as cold and/or stoic. While it may have come across that way to some people, it was merely my coping mechanism. I didn't know any other way I could possibly have endured such an ordeal.

The service began. A man I didn't know—perhaps a volunteer

congregant—positioned himself with a video camera on a tripod in the rear of the sanctuary. I am grateful he had the incredible foresight to videotape the entire event, so it would exist for posterity on VHS and later be transcribed. After the service, he personally handed the tape to me.

For the most part, William sat in his stroller, while Rachael sat close by my side. After about the first twenty minutes, she grew bored with the speeches and whispered something in my ear before leaving her seat and heading outside. Beside us in the front row were Jerry, Jaci, Roberta, Michelle, and Steven. Eva sat in the same row as us but across the aisle.

A clergy member (likely the synagogue's cantor) initiated the proceedings with a touching rendition of the Bread song "If a Picture Paints a Thousand Words." Rabbi Krantz ushered in the speeches:

> *I was not privileged to know Mark during his lifetime. I wish that I had come to know him to create a memory for him, which is our task today. Our sanctuary would not be so full if Mark had not lived such an extraordinary life.*
>
> *We gather underneath the darkest shadow that I can remember in my thirty-year career. I can explain neither good nor evil. The role of religion is not to explain what cannot be explained. Judaism is not the book of why, but of what to do— to be humble in the presence of extraordinary good or extraordinary evil. . . . It instructs us on how to live, how to mourn, and to begin to remember. We will create for Mark what will be his memory. We must choose life and orient ourselves toward living.*

Allan was the first speaker after the rabbi. He wore a suit and tie and his usual glasses. He lumbered toward the front. When he reached the podium, he placed two hands on it to steady himself.

He paused, sucking in a deep breath. He brought notes but had committed most of his speech to memory and addressed the audience in a strong and steady voice.

> *It's difficult to try to put into words somebody you know ten hours a day, five days a week, year after year.*
>
> *I'm going to share some of Mark's many fine traits with you and how they permeated his home life, his school life, the DA's office, and his life in college. A life described by [his] loads of friends who sent me emails.*
>
> *Two weeks ago, I wrote Mark's nomination [for] partnership to the firm. It was easy to write. I'm glad I made the decision to show it to Mark. He was proud and happy ... and then asked to make a couple of corrections and additions.*
>
> *[Audience laughter]*
>
> *I wish I still had it, but it went down in the building [the World Trade Center]. It was very detailed, and I wish I could remember it all so I could give it to Juliette. The biggest section had to do with his morality and his ethics and what I thought he could do for the firm in years to come. He was future-oriented, and I thought he could be a rock and anchor for people because he had the kinds of traits that you could hang on to. He was* never *rattled; he was* always *calm.*
>
> *When I spoke to people who told me about that last day, [they said] Mark was calm—and I'm sure he was. And his calmness came from the fact that he was one of the brightest people I have ever met. That came out in the emails I sent out to clients, adversaries, and co-defendants. I asked [people] to give me an impression [of him]. I got so many, they filled up a three-ring binder. . . .*
>
> Everybody *considered Mark a friend.* Everybody *thought he was the brightest person in the room.* Everybody *thought*

he had a great sense of humor. . . . Everybody said Mark was helpful. This is one of the traits [that led to us wanting him] to be a partner. . . .

He would take things that I wrote and make them magically better. He would get things organized before they happened and polish them along the way. He was rare in that he was smart but didn't have an ego. He recognized that people didn't have what he had by virtue of experience or training, and he would figure out [how] he was going to help them.

I am sorry that he didn't get to become partner—but he was in spirit. I'd like to think that I was his mentor—but he was mine. He taught me things I didn't know. . . .

In doing what we do as lawyers—which is sometimes difficult—we have to depend on the people we work with and trust their judgment, intellect, morals, ethics, and ability to get things done. This is what made Mark such an outstanding lawyer. These traits also made Mark so easy to befriend.

However, Mark was more than just a lawyer; he was a proud family man and let you know just how much his wife and children meant to him. He will sorely be missed in our world. . . .

Another [person, a competitive attorney] wrote the following about Mark:

"I thought Mark was a person who generally liked people—no matter who they were or where they were from. He liked to talk, he liked to joke, he liked to be with people. Mark could fill up a room with his personality—a little sly, a little funny, always a twinkle in his eye. Mark loved the law, and this is probably the reason we became friends. He loved the rough and tumble of the law—the jostling, the sporting nature. Throughout the three years we spent working on 'latex glove' cases, we shared the competitive thrill of being adversaries, pulling punches and protecting our clients."

My loss of Mark is a friend in the law. We often talked about being in court for the next forty years in massive tort litigation. This year, working on latex gloves—next year, who knows? He was a man whose judgment I could trust, whose instincts were sound, [and] whose intelligence was unmatched.

The law lost a lot when we lost Mark. He was a great intellectual [and] a persuasive trial lawyer at the dawn of what promised to be a long and brilliant career. I will always carry in my heart Mark's memory. And I vow to do my best as a lawyer in his memory.

People in the firm genuinely looked up to him. He was truly one of our intellectual bean sprouts that was growing and growing and growing. He was one of those lawyers who knew where he [was going] and, I'm telling you, he had goals. . . .

We recognized he was a builder; *he knew* how *to get places*—tactfully, *nicely, as a friend. I'm hoping that this is something that rubbed off on me and [that I] carry with me. I hope Mark's calmness rubs off.*

He was really *a good* man.

I was then called up to the *bima* (the platform in a synagogue from which a service is typically led). I didn't think I was particularly nervous, but I knew I didn't sound like my usual self. My voice shook as I spoke in a soft, monotone voice. I had several handwritten pages of my prepared speech available; I read most of it and improvised a bit as well. I addressed the audience directly at times—looking up and out—although I didn't focus on any face in particular.

I wanted to speak today to give a full understanding of what a special person my husband was. I want to let everyone know that he had such a love for this community, this town of Armonk. He would be so proud of the generous and gracious ways you have supported me and our family during this difficult time. In the weeks before he died, he was working on something concerning the safety of our children on the street where we live. I'm hoping we can see this become a reality.

Now I'll talk about our lives together. From the day I met him in the summer of 1986, he was a man with a plan. He had unusual confidence and trust in himself, and he lived his life with focus and with clear goals—and the amazing thing was that he was able to make them a reality.

We met when I was only eighteen and he was nineteen. It became clear to me that, once we got to know each other, he had our whole lives planned out. At the time, that was quite a lot for me to hear. I chuckled a little bit and said, "How can you make these sorts of plans?"—but I just knew in the back of my mind that what he was saying was true and meant to be.

I also wanted to tell you that he proved to be a wonderful husband. In these eight years he was always supportive. He told me how wonderful I was every day and told anybody who would listen what a terrific wife he had. He never took me for granted and helped me value myself.

Recently, when I was feeling overwhelmed by my life and having two small kids, I was questioning myself and asking, "Am I doing the right things?" and "Am I bringing value to my life and theirs?" His words were so powerful: "Your children are going to grow up soon enough and they won't need you like they do now—so, when that time comes, you will be able to look back on these years and be proud of yourself, because you raised them. You are the person I want raising the kids, not someone else."

He was a man of only thirty-four years, but he was very wise. He was also a wonderful father and the kids adored him. He didn't have much physical time with them during the week, so he would playfully refer to himself as "weekend daddy." He worked a long day and came home between seven thirty and eight on most nights. But he would spend that time with the kids before he even ate dinner, changed clothes, or unwound in front of the TV. Usually, he would wait until they were asleep before he did anything to relax.

Weekends, of course, were entirely family oriented. Recently, he saw that the movie The Family Man was out on video. He became all excited and said, "That movie is about me." I should go out and buy it for him. I've been a little busy lately, but still plan to buy it. I think it's something the kids need to see.

There's something else I need to say. People have been asking how we seem so strong as a family—or we seem to be—and, with some careful thought, I think I have an explanation for it. I know personally that Mark was always my strength, and he's the one giving the strength now. I do feel his presence a lot, and it calms and reassures me.

In closing, I want to share the last words we heard from him. He made a phone call to my house and, unfortunately, I didn't answer the phone, my sister did. He said to her, "Tell Juliette that I'm okay and that I'm coming home."

And . . . I'd like to think that wherever he is now, he is okay and that he's gone home.

Alan, Mark's best friend from college, followed me.

Mark was my friend. Friendship was very important to him. [We belonged to] Theta Chi Fraternity, which had the motto: "lending a helping hand." I don't think there was anyone who practiced and understood being a helping hand better than Mark.

It's impossible to come up with one word or example to truly *illustrate the depth Mark cared for his friends . . . [he once took] the time out of his hectic schedule to visit a mutual friend of ours who was seriously injured and in the hospital.*

When Mark's friends had problems, they became his problems. He did whatever he could to help us. When I was looking for a job, Mark—without my knowledge—would talk to the recruiters . . . get all the information of the firms . . . [and] then he would call me up and say, "These are the firms that you should be sending resumes to. [They] are looking for lawyers right now . . ." When Mark's friends were successful, he shared their joy. Mark never felt diminished by somebody else's success. He wanted people close to him to succeed and did what he could to help them.

Mark never feared adversity. At work, he wanted the hard cases. When we worked together at Barbri [a bar exam preparation course], Mark was always willing to answer the difficult questions for the students who called in. In his calm, clear way, he would go over it for the student until they were reassured that they understood the answer and they had what they needed to study for the Bar. . . .

Last week, I was talking to somebody [who] remarked that Mark was the kind of person who made a lasting impression on everybody he came into contact with. I've been thinking about that for a while and it's really true. Mark mattered: from college, when we were debate partners, to the DA's office where we argued together in court, to recently, where we gave lectures for the CLE [continuing legal education] for newly admitted lawyers.

Mark was my fraternity brother, he was my teammate, he was my partner—but, most of all, he was my best friend. I love him and not a day is going to go by where Mark will not be missed.

Jaci was the next speaker. She wore a simple black dress. She rose from her seat in the front row and approached me to offer her support before stepping toward to the *bima*. She turned around to acknowledge the clergy, put on her glasses, and spoke in a cracked voice while clutching a tissue.

I thought long and hard about what to say here—if anything at all. I still don't know if I'll be able to say what I want without totally breaking down in the middle. I couldn't really think of the right words to describe what I'm really feeling about this horrible tragedy...

The biggest problem is that I can't or won't think of Mark in the past tense because I truly feel he is still with us—in spirit, in heart, in soul. [Mark's heart] always knew the right thing to do. He always did the right thing.

There was not a mean bone in his body. His spirit will always be with us. Every time I hear Rachael and William, I'll think of Mark's spirit. Mark's soul is with us everywhere. It will stay with us, always.

Eric, my son, said something very poignant to Rob the other day. He said that he misses Uncle Mark's great big hugs. And he's right. Everything about Mark was great and big—his hugs, his laughter, his good will.

Juliette, I want you to know that Rob and I will always be here for you and the kids. I hope to strengthen our relationship. I know that's what Mark would have wanted. Eric and Rachael adore each other, they are great friends.

Mark: I just want to say I love you, my baby brother, you will always be in my heart.

Michelle followed Jaci. She was also attired in a black dress with a pin on her lapel. She walked quickly and with determination to the *bima*. Once there, she unfolded her prepared speech, which she read with great effort through her sniffles.

> As most of you already know, I am Mark's twin sister. I have fond and loving memories of Mark, as most of you do. Being a twin is the most wonderful experience anyone could ever imagine. I can't even begin to describe it. I had a built-in best friend for life.
>
> Mark and I used to joke about how we were born. We made up a story of how we were playing chess in the womb. Not checkers, chess. I was winning and Mark got so angry that he walked out in a huff and was born.
>
> *[Audience laughter]*
>
> Ten minutes later, I followed him. This is how it worked for so many years. I was always running after him.
>
> I have such fond memories growing up. I loved the joint birthday parties and the pink and blue cakes. We shared the same group of friends throughout our childhood and teenage years. It was never uncool to hang out with him. I loved going to school with Mark and sharing so many classes. I remember when he called on me to be his debate partner in high school because [I was] all Mark could find.
>
> I believe the competition we had growing up drove me to excel. I remember going to camp Wah-Nee, where we would trade comic books for mom's care packages. We both won camper of the week the same week.
>
> [I remember] fixing his hair for formals. He and I both had a time with his hair.
>
> *[Audience laughter]*
>
> There's so much to say. I loved his kindness, his generosity, his goofy smile—which William has—his laughter, and his

sense of humor. I've been so fortunate to get closer to him and Juliette over the last few years. With Mark, I could talk about anything, and we shared so much. He really understood me and helped me through some hard times.

He was such a great listener. I promise to always be there for Juliette, Rachael, and William, as Mark would want it.

May God be with you Mark, I love you always.

Steven was the last to speak. Wearing a dress shirt and blazer, he took his time approaching the stage. He arranged his papers on the pulpit and studied them for a few moments. He wiped sweat from his brow with his sleeve and continued in a steady tone.

I want to begin [by discussing] such an unconscionable event [9/11]. What has transpired in the last two weeks is beyond catastrophic. For my family and for the entire world. Speaking to a close friend the other day, I can only describe the pain on many levels—emotional pain, familial pain, moral pain, and political pain. The sense of emptiness has left a void in my heart that leaves me breathless. The inability to try to reconcile the events of [that] Tuesday keeps anger in my mind and my heart.

In recent weeks, we have received mail from all over the world, people we haven't spoken to in twenty or thirty years. The outpouring from our community is astounding. Yet every person I speak to utters the same four words: "What can I say . . ."

The answer is always the same, there's much to talk about, yet nothing to say. On Tuesday September 11, 2001, my life as I knew it came to a screeching halt. American Airlines Flight 11 slammed into Tower One of the World Trade Center. At 8:48 a.m., my mother was watching television in her apartment. She immediately called my brother on the eighty-fifth floor of Tower

Two. He said he was safe and that he was leaving. In typical Mark fashion, he began to calm his coworkers, comfort the staff, and methodically pack up his essentials.

After all, he was probably anticipating not being back at the office for a few days. Amidst the obvious chaos, Mark was ensuring the safety of others while continuing to wrap up his work. Simply doing his job with pride and dignity. The consummate team player. He was working with a level of commitment that was instilled by our parents. Or, as [Mr.] Spock—Mark loved Star Trek and all science fiction—said, "The needs of the many outweigh the needs of the few."

The irony of the situation is overwhelming. Imagine the act that resonated from a loyal, unselfish individual ricocheting back at the cost of your life. Those actions typify Mark. My baby brother, all 6'3" of him. Sweeter than sweet. Kinder than kind. Salt of the earth. He possessed the heart of a lion and the soul of a content, humble man. From May 9, 1967—the day he was born—it was a mitzvah (blessing). Jacqueline and I were blessed with not one but two siblings. A boy and a girl. Mark and Michelle. M and M.

As a child, Mark was a compassionate and caring one. Amongst the four of us, he was the referee. The mediator.

After graduation from the State University of Albany with honors, Mark attended New York University School of Law, one of our country's finest institutions. Following his tenure as an assistant district attorney in New York, Mark entered private practice. The dignity and pride that drove Mark was always reflected in his work. We had just gone out for a quiet dinner alone, the four of us—Juliette, Mark, myself, and Barbara—when Mark announced he had been nominated for partnership. How proud we were of my thirty-four-year-old brother!

My wife, Barbara, who first met Mark when he was

sixteen, said, "I love your brother, Mark—his heart is gold."

To those of us who survive my brother: We must feel the pain and sorrow as I do from this tragic loss.

Mom, Dad: I can't even begin to fathom the state of your emotions. Gaining strength from the thought of what a wholesome, loving man you raised. His intelligence was only overshadowed by his sensitivity. He was articulate, handsome, and an absolute sweetheart. The kind of guy you want to bring home to your parents.

To his wife, Juliette—whom he often referred to as Jules—you were the only woman he ever loved, and his love for you was unyielding. Juliette, he was proud of you, proud of the children you gave him, proud of the home you made for him, and proud of the friendship you shared. Mark's greatest love of all was his two children. He was the Pied Piper [to] all the children. Uncle Mark treated all the kids as if they were his own. He had the energy of a youngster and the patience of a saint.

William: There was no one more proud than your father [when he had] a son. To carry on his name and all the traditions that follow. Your dad was proud of being Jewish and couldn't wait to instill the principles that come with being a Jewish man. Nothing brought him more joy [than] the first time you were all able to go to synagogue.

Rachael: I know all too well what a special bond between father and a daughter can be. He cherished all the time you spent together—Saturday morning coffee runs [and] those quiet moments when he'd read to you. Make no mistake about it, I will make sure you and William never forget. Rachael—you do, however, possess a gift that is unique to you and your brother. His spirit is in your blood and in your heart. And if you feel you have forgotten him, simply go to your reflection, look into your eyes, and you will see your father.

As for me, I [now appreciate] the expression "I am for my brother." He was my best man. I recall having to move out of my apartment in Philadelphia, and I called and asked my parents, "How do I pack up my things and move back home?" The answer was simple: "I'll send your brother."

[Audience laughter]

I can't begin to describe what I shared with Mark in my entire life—from every holiday, to every birthday, to every Giants game, [to every] playoff game, and to the Super Bowl. As I sat in synagogue this past week during the Rosh Hashanah holiday and the New Year 5762—how eerie it was not having Mark next to me. Out of all the moments we shared, it was those special moments where we communicated through our eyes without even speaking a single note. The type of nonverbal body language that can only be shared by those special relationships in life. Two close friends, a set of twins, a husband and wife, and, yes, two brothers. So, on the second day of Rosh Hashanah, I solemnly went to synagogue—just my father and me. We left one seat open between us, perhaps involuntarily leaving it for Mark. And, as the service came to a close, we got to the Aleinu [a closing prayer that signifies "It is our obligation to praise God"]. Dad looked at me and said nothing. For Mark loved the Aleinu—not for what it said but for what it meant. The Aleinu signifies the end of the service and the beginning of the afternoon.

[Audience laughter]

It symbolized completion. It signified [it was] time to move on. He gave me that look that can only be shared by those close special people in your life.

But this is not the end. Rather, this is the beginning. The beginning for all of us to share our feelings about Mark on [an] even a higher level. Time to cherish those moments that Mark *has inscribed on each of our lives.*

Mark: May your spirit live on in all of us for ever and ever. God bless you.

The memorial seemed so surreal. It was as if this was all happening to someone else. While I had steeled myself and didn't cry during speeches, I noticed several other people sobbing—those who knew Mark intimately, as well as total strangers. I heard murmurs of "It's such a tragedy," "It's so sad," and "He was so young" throughout the proceedings.

Not everyone was so sweet and sensitive, however. It became evident to me that some people say shameful, judgmental things when they are in emotional anguish. I was later told about the following stinging comment made regarding me: "Look—her husband is dead, and she doesn't even care."

Considering the circumstances and short notice, the event went smoothly, except for my having to deal with a few awkward conversations afterward. I understand. Many people feel they have to say *something* and genuinely want to help me feel better, so they recite the usual cliches: "I'm so sorry," "He was a good man," "It was a beautiful service...." Others ended up saying peculiar things. A few lacked commonsense and said insensitive things such as the following middle-aged woman who broke down in tears: "Oh, you poor thing! Such a tragedy!"

Huh? Why am I consoling her?

Another offered: "You're young, you're attractive, you'll be just fine."

I know what she's implying! How could she suggest a "replacement" at a time like this?

The gravesite ceremony at the cemetery directly followed the memorial. The rabbi performed a traditional service and pinned a black cloth on the top garments worn by the immediate family of mourners (Mark's parents, his siblings, and me).

The one obvious issue was that we didn't have any physical remains to place in the coffin. Jerry felt strongly about putting his own *tallit* (a white prayer shawl worn during Jewish services) in the casket instead of Mark's. He'd realized that the tallit Mark had personally received at his Bar Mitzvah would be of greater significance when it would be handed down to one of his children down the road. Roberta placed a photo of Mark along with the tallit. My contributions were some family photographs, including our wedding picture.

We watched the casket lower into the ground. Once it was in position, we shoveled dirt on top of it, as is Jewish custom.

I wish that one day we'll have a burial with more than just mementos. I owe him that.

In the days following the cemetery service, Jerry, Eva, and I attended a support meeting for 9/11 families in Westchester, New York. It was a well-intended effort by a social service agency to offer surviving adult family members the opportunity to provide mutual support and share their stories and feelings, as they might best relate to each other's experiences. Someone facilitated the event but, for the most part, attendees just vented. They expressed pain, frustration, heartache, and doom and gloom. Some blamed God.

"My life is over . . ."

"Where was God that day that he allowed this to happen?"

"Everything is gone . . ."

"I used to have faith—but not anymore . . ."

I realized I didn't fit into this group at all. While I respected their perspectives, I didn't agree with them in terms of my life. The gathering ended up being a negative, depressing experience. At this point I didn't think I needed to connect with other 9/11 families—and certainly not with these particular widows. I was just as traumatized as they were, but I was not willing to accept that it was the end of my life. I wanted as much consistency and normalcy for my family and me as possible and resolved to continue leaning on my existing support system.

Maybe these conversations took place too soon for me. I remained in shock, lost in a fog ...

I was continually amazed by the extent some people went out of their way to help ease my situation. The local Jewish Community Center (JCC) arranged for a sign-up where meals were sent over to my house. This continued until I told them I no longer had the space to store it all or the people to feed. My parents went back home to Long Island after about two weeks. The preschool offered to waive their fees for my kids (which I politely declined). I was concerned at the time that our family might be treated differently if I were to accept. A student named Tess from Fairfield University in Connecticut volunteered to come over and babysit every week; she refused to accept any money. I was also connected with Jennifer, who worked as a housekeeper for a few local families. She became indispensable to me and the children, just by her warm presence alone.

That was the tip of the iceberg. Local and national charities mobilized and started to disperse funds to our family, as well as others. This money gave me peace of mind, as I could put the scary question of "How will I support my family?" off for a while longer.

Meanwhile, Jerry was already focused on the future: He started a college fund for his grandchildren, and he created the Mark Brisman Memorial Scholarship Fund at New York University School of

Law. Also at the law school, Rick—Mark's college friend—joined with other 1992 alumni to create a scholarship award in his honor.

The cards and letters from total strangers flooded my mailbox. Agencies dedicated to 9/11 sent us gifts from people all around the country. These tokens provided such comfort, as well as joy for the kids who enjoyed opening these "surprises." Among these were a small patchwork quilt, a pillow doll (whose head allowed for a photo or drawing of your "person" to serve as its face), and many books of a spiritual nature.

Jerry continued to amaze and impress me. He became something of a financial advisor and personal secretary, managing all business matters and payments. He helped sort out my banking and tax situations, which weren't all that difficult because Mark kept such organized records. He filled out the police reports, the missing person's report, and the death certificate paperwork on my behalf.

One evening, while Jerry and Eva spent time with me in my living room, we all broke down and cried about Mark. "If I only it had been *me* instead of him," Jerry sobbed in a rare moment of letting his guard down. "I would have traded places with him in a minute."

Financially, we were okay for a time. I couldn't complain about any treatment I received. Mark's law firm paid Mark's salary and continued his benefits (health insurance) through the end of the year, which only had three and a half months left. After that, I went on COBRA for health insurance.

As the weeks went by, I tried my best to establish a normal life for my children and me. They continued with preschool, and I went about my business maintaining the house, preparing meals, driving the kids to and from events, and providing as much love and attention to them as I could to fill the enormous gap left by Mark's absence.

For the most part, my strategy worked—right up until Monday mornings when I dropped the kids off at school. As part of normal chitchat, other parents would talk about what they had done over the weekends—where they had gone out to dinner with their spouses, what movies they had just seen together, and so on. For me, the weekends were devoid of such simple pleasures without Mark around.

Often, I faced uncomfortable encounters. It seemed that wherever I went—the supermarket, the gym, or just walking around town—acquaintances who otherwise wouldn't have stopped to give me the time of day now waved and shouted encouraging things at me. People felt they had to seek me out and strike up conversations, which often turned strange.

"Look at you—you're *so skinny!*"

Of course I am! I've barely eaten in two weeks. If your husband had died, you'd look like this, too! It's a great weight-loss plan!

I heard the same old comments over and over again: "How are you holding up?" "How are the kids doing?" and on and on. I could always sense when people were talking about me off to the side. They had a certain look, as if they were saying, "Oh, *that's her* . . ." I disliked being singled out and being on the receiving end of any kind of pity.

For the upcoming end-of-the-year holiday cards, I impulsively decided to have professional photos taken of my children instead of the usual candid snaps I normally sent out. It seemed like a moment in time I needed to capture. Of course, young kids aren't always cooperative during posed photographs, so the photographer had to manage them a bit. He struggled to coax them into a happy mood with the usual silly faces and voices. When that didn't work, he uttered, "Let's have a big smile for Daddy."

Unbeknownst to the photographer, it was the single worst thing he could have said to them at that moment. I held back the tears and elected not to inform him of our situation. Why start trouble with someone who had made an innocent remark?

Rachael and William seemed to be working things out in their own individual ways. During playdates with friends, Rachael occasionally blurted out things like "Did you know my daddy is gone?"

Every so often, she initiated dark conversations out of the blue. "You're going to die before me, aren't you, Mommy?"

I knew where she was going with this and had to ease her worries. From her perspective: If she'd lost her father, maybe I would be the next to go? "Don't worry. I plan to live a long, healthy life. I'm not going anywhere."

"How old was Daddy when he died?"

"Thirty-four."

"Since Daddy is in heaven, can I talk to him?"

"Sure you can. You can speak to him by praying . . . like when we go to temple."

"When are we going to temple again? I want to pray and talk to Daddy."

William was a different story. Who knows what goes on in a two-year-old boy's mind when such an important figure in his life suddenly vanishes? I noticed that his personality changed from that point onward. He became more sensitive and aware of when others—especially Rachael and me—were troubled. He always came across as empathetic, present, and supportive. He didn't seem to have any inclination to act out or cause trouble, as if he didn't want to risk getting anyone upset.

One evening, when William was two and a half and had begun speaking sentences with regularity, he told me that his father had appeared to him in a dream. "Dad was with us," he conveyed in a composed tone. He didn't seem disturbed by it; in fact, it might have been comforting to him. The most difficult part for me was that I had shared a similar dream the night before. The odd coincidence was almost too much for me to bear, although I was somehow able to prevent myself from breaking down in front of him.

Once the immediate and overpowering shock and awe of 9/11 started to wear off, family members began to offer advice. My parents became convinced that staying in my house in Armonk was a bad choice for their grandchildren and me, as it stirred up too many sad memories. "Why don't you sell the house and move closer to us?"

There was no chance of that happening at that time. My kids had close friends and so did I. I considered moving away as a detriment, as it risked breaking up our family routines and sending out the impression that we were fleeing.

My little family moments, such as the kids' first birthdays without their father, were often the most bittersweet. When Rachael rode her bicycle up and down the street, I could picture Mark proudly standing right behind her with his wide smile. When I went for walks with either or both kids in the early evening, I imagined him pulling up in the driveway in his car and joining us.

The year after 9/11 was a blur—an alternate reality. I remained tightly bound in my cocoon with Rachael and William, and shut out as much of the outside world as I could. I thought I was moving forward and healing, and saw no reason to involve myself in anything related to that horrifying day.

Then something unforeseen occurred: My perspective changed, and my life veered in a different direction.

Chapter Fourteen

Help Me, Rhonda!

Armonk, New York
October 2002–July 2004

On an ordinary afternoon while having an afterschool snack, Rachael matter-of-factly made the following remark: "Mom, did you know that William and I are the only kids without a dad?"

I was taken aback. Everything seemed fine with her until that moment; she'd seemed safe and comfortable.

Have I missed something?

"That's not true," I countered. "A lot of people lost their dads on 9/11—you and William aren't the only ones. In fact, an overwhelming number of people who died that day were dads. We just don't know any of those other families personally."

Rachael considered my explanation and it seemed to satisfy her, but her question stuck with me. My family and I had done everything we could to support the children post 9/11—but were we enough? It occurred to me that I couldn't take a chance of some lingering emotional trauma, and that the protective bubble I had created had outlived its usefulness. I could no longer shield my children from the reality of what happened to our family. It was time to begin the conversation and prepare them for whatever was to come.

The natural solution was to reach out beyond our current support system.

I called the Westchester Jewish Community Services and asked if they still offered any counseling for us. A good amount of time had passed since 9/11, so it crossed my mind that the spigot for nonprofit family support might have been turned off. Fortunately, this wasn't the case; they continued to provide individual and group therapy for adults and children.

At the time, I knew nothing about therapy and initially thought of it as transactional; we would show up and receive a service, much like a hair salon. We'd go in looking like a mess and come out glowing and beautiful. I expected answers and reassurances right away, especially regarding whether my kids would be damaged and/or if Rachael would have issues with relationships later, since she'd lost her father when she was so young. As I discovered, I couldn't have been more incorrect about how the therapy process works.

I set up separate biweekly meetings for Rachael and myself at the same time with different professionals. Rachael looked forward to the visits since she had a child therapist of her own and received special one-on-one attention. Based on her age, the pair played games and did puzzles, during which time the therapist slid in casual conversations about Mark. There were no major visible breakthroughs that I was made aware of, but Rachael always seemed to come away having had a good time.

As for me, I lucked into the perfect therapist: a social worker named Rhonda: a petite woman in her forties who applied ample makeup, wore stylish clothes and jewelry, and had brown frizzy hair. Rhonda's nasal voice reminded me of the TV sitcom comedienne Fran Drescher of *The Nanny* fame. Her windowless office wasn't much to speak of, consisting of a desk, two chairs, industrial carpet, and sparse wall décor. Although the environment wasn't what I had envisioned, I expected Rhonda to have solutions to all my problems.

I dove in right away asking for reassurances that my daughter wasn't going to have a lifetime of issues down the road. Her response took me by surprise. "That all depends on *you*."

"*Me*? What do you mean?"

"How she feels about things is determined by your messaging," she explained. "The situation is enormous and painful, but you weren't abandoned by your husband, nor did your daughter witness any abuse in the home. That makes a difference. If *you* don't act bitter or resentful regarding the opposite sex, she has no reason to have any issues in this regard. Unless . . . is she showing any symptoms of concerning behavior?"

"No . . ."

"Then she's probably going to be fine."

I somehow didn't think this was enough. I couldn't believe it was so simple and within my control. "If I find a 'replacement' father soon, would that help?"

Rhonda took a breath before answering. "Listen, Juliette, your daughter will *always* have one father and that's it. There is no way for you to 'fix' Mark's not being around. You don't have to force things. While you have control over what you say about him and how you handle your conversations with her, there is nothing you can do to 'solve' his loss for her—or for yourself. Keep in mind: The fact that you are widowed doesn't mean your *life* is widowed."

Rhonda had given me a great deal of food for thought. I didn't have to panic about Rachael's future—or mine. The situation wasn't nearly as dire as I'd thought.

In addition to the emotional discomfort I'd felt hearing other couples discuss what they had done over the weekend together or as families, there was always that lingering, unstated gap left by

Mark's absence. Birthdays, holidays, and other special events were blistering reminders for me that he wasn't there with us to share in the happy times I know he would have loved so much. Still, we were happy to be part of Brisman family gatherings.

There were also the practical things one doesn't expect. Like most preschool boys his age, William loved Legos and other building type toys that had a million little pieces requiring expert assembly. This had been completely in Mark's purview, and I struggled figuring out how to put things together. I broke down in tears late one at night after the kids were in bed. This was one of the rare times I became frustrated and felt sorry for myself. Out of sheer desperation and not wanting to look like a failure in front of my son, I read the hell out of those directions and put those damn things together. Sure, they were only toys, but I never felt so accomplished and proud of myself once they were assembled!

Another thing I never considered: Mark had been the family driver and liked doing it. I was suddenly the primary person taxiing the kids everywhere; not just to and from school and their extracurricular activities, but also to relatives' homes in Long Island (my parents), Pennsylvania (Jerry and Eva), and Boston (my sister). I was a decent driver, but it scared me to think I was solely responsible for the kids' safety in the backseat. In the beginning, these longer trips frightened me.

What if something happens?

The visits were well worth it. The kids and I needed the unconditional support of our families. My parents became like second parents to Rachael and William. Even though my mom was still working full-time at the library, she made herself available on her days off. They were youngish grandparents with boundless energy who were up for just about anything—even town fairs and other loud and raucous kiddie play places where we'd split up and follow the kids around. Then, after a full and exhausting day, we'd enjoy

Grammy J's delicious dinners. When she would inevitably overstep her boundaries—such as scolding me for not serving the kids meals "hot enough"—I'd have to remind her that I was the "mom #1 in charge" when it came to decision-making and parenting.

My semi-retired father, who became known as "Poppy," was the disciplinarian grandfather. He operated out of worry and didn't hesitate to raise his voice. Whenever my kids acted out and were being naughty, just the threat of informing Poppy about their misbehavior was enough to reel them back in line. He had his fun side, too, introducing William to The Shadow and other comic book heroes of his own childhood. Poppy, the consummate tough guy throughout this challenging time, was reduced to tears only once. Around her fifth birthday, Rachael was scheduled for a follow up with a cardiologist at the children's hospital in Valhalla, her first appointment in several years to check up on her heart defect. Poppy insisted on accompanying us, despite my efforts to persuade him that I was fine going alone. After the echocardiogram tests were complete, the doctor sat us down in his office to give us the report. "Rachael's heart defect has completely closed, and no further care is needed," he informed us with a satisfied smile. "Your daughter is free to live a normal healthy life."

My dad's emotional outburst was immediate. He thanked a higher power through his tears and suggested Mark may have somehow intervened to help produce this miracle.

A whole other dynamic developed with Jerry and Eva, whose remote lakefront home felt to us like we had been transported to a Zen-like other world. Jerry, now fully retired, became vested in being a grandfather. He often took both kids out fishing on his pontoon boat, where they mostly caught "sunnies" (sunfish). My kids would swim from the boat to explore small "deserted islands"—small rocky patches in the middle of the lake. On their return, they'd report back their discoveries to their eager grandparents. Jerry found a kindred spirit in his grandson and was able to draw out the curious mind that lay just underneath the surface of the energetic little boy. He became an important role model, providing William with the special one-on-one time he desperately wanted.

Jerry also enriched Rachael's intellect, challenging her with new "big girl" vocabulary words, such as *narcissistic*, *impressionable*, and *deleterious*. In the evenings, we dressed up in our finest and headed to "the club," where the staff and Jerry and Eva's friends treated us like pseudo-celebrities. The kids felt like big shots ordering fancy drinks (Shirley Temples), which were the rewards (or bribes) for behaving themselves through lengthy meals.

In early 2002, Jerry and Eva treated us to a trip to Disney's Magic Kingdom in Orlando, Florida, where we attempted to escape our sadness for a while.

Meanwhile, Roberta enjoyed her time with the grandchildren. Although she was still battling cancer, she made time for the kids during her many visits to Westchester. One of her favorite outings was to the candy store in town, where she allowed them to indulge in whatever treats their hearts desired. When Roberta dropped the kids off at home, they excitedly presented me with overloaded bags filled with colorful confections that could have lasted for months. I didn't have the heart to tell my mother-in-law to use moderation, as I knew she enjoyed the shopping spree just as much—if not more than—the kids.

I celebrated my first post-9/11 birthday at a Hibachi restaurant with the family.

Unfortunately, Roberta's illness continued to progress rapidly, and she declined to the point of needing home health care. She passed away in December 2002.

To fill the parental void of their father's absence, I tended to overindulge the kids at times; the three of us were regular visitors to Toys "R" Us toy store in White Plains. William modeled himself as a mini–Captain Feathersword—a character from *The Wiggles* kiddie TV show. On Sunday afternoons, we stalked the store aisles for items he didn't yet possess. Before long, he had a toy chest full of assorted weaponry. Dave, a neighbor and close friend who had three daughters (and may have wished he'd had a son), knew of William's interest and loved to challenge him to "duels." The two would engage in combat, with William draping his blankie over one shoulder and attacking his adversary with the plastic or foam weapon of his choosing.

It was easy for me to think "I don't need a guy around," but, clearly, men like Dave made a positive difference in our lives. Of course, there wasn't always a male present while William was potty training, which complicated things for me. I had been deluded into thinking boys could just pee in the woods, which seemed less stressful than carting William into the ladies' room. I learned my lesson when a fellow playground mom saw William urinating on a nearby tree and called me out for it. From then on, William used indoor bathrooms like every other toddler.

William was not at all interested in sports at the time, which worried me. I felt guilty that he would be at a disadvantage being raised by a mother who wasn't into that kind of thing. I tried to put on a good show by putting the Giants football game on and imitating the commentary I'd heard Mark utter over the years. He saw right through me and didn't want any part of it.

A few times, I insisted we play catch in the yard. I grabbed Mark's old baseball mitt, and we'd toss a ball around. After a few minutes or so, William would grow bored and ask me why we had to play catch. He didn't care for T-ball, gymnastics, or even soccer, although he tried them all. He was drawn to his comic books and their good versus evil scenarios. He also had a fascination with earth sciences, weather patterns, and natural disasters. After a while, I accepted the reality that athletics wouldn't be part of his life.

Rachael found her own outlet, performing on stage—dancing, singing, and acting. She was fearless and relished the spotlight. She could project her voice louder than most kids her age and was impossible to ignore with her enormous brown eyes, lush ringlets of chestnut brown hair, and her father's mega-watt smile. The directors at the Theater Arts Workshop, a local children's theater company, entrusted Rachael with lead roles in *Peter Pan*, *The Sound of Music*, and *Annie*.

A year and a half went by without any developments related to 9/11. Then . . . I received a call from the NYPD informing me that remains had been positively identified as Mark's through DNA matching. I couldn't believe it. Something physical of him had remained, after all. They believed it was a fragment of bone from his leg.

Not knowing what to do, I contacted Rabbi Krantz. He suggested that we add the bone to Mark's grave and say a few prayers over it. The cemetery was contacted, and they agreed to our request to reopen the plot. Rather than raise and open the casket, the remains were placed in a small wooden box and added on top of it. I declined the option of looking at the fragment and chose not to make a ceremony out of it. Rabbi Krantz and I were the only ones present as the box was lowered onto the casket. He recited a few psalms before the grave was refilled.

Another touch of closure occurred at around this time. A prominent attorney named Robert Kellner contacted Jerry to offer his representation to help us establish our claim with the September 11th Victim Compensation Fund. This wasn't by random happenstance. Mr. Kellner, who had partnered with attorney Kenneth Feinberg—Special Master of Fund and former Chief of

Staff to Senator Ted Kennedy—knew of Mark from participating in the Moot Court simulations at NYU, which had also been taped. Mark's name must have caught Mr. Kellner's eye on a 9/11 list, and he personally searched for a family member, ultimately landing upon Jerry, who put the lawyer in direct contact with me by phone.

Mr. Kellner impressed me from the start: He was no-nonsense and knew his stuff. I was encouraged by the extra personal attention he was providing to my family, which we never sought. Mr. Kellner respected Mark from having known him in a professional setting and, in his words, wanted "to make sure you and your children are properly taken care of."

His efforts paid off. Mark's 9/11 settlement payment arrived before the end of 2004. In retrospect, the three-year wait was not a long time—especially when one considers how long it usually takes for bureaucracies to operate, green light payments, and execute. From my perspective—though I can't speak to anyone else's situation—I can't complain about how the US government handled 9/11. They did right by our family.

Gradually, I started to come out of my shell and become involved in community events and 9/11 initiatives. I read a poem—"We Remember Them," by Sylvan Kamens and Rabbi Jack Riemer—at the first annual 9/11 memorial event for Westchester County. Around this time, an employee from the Westchester County Executive's Office contacted me to see if I would like to join a group consisting of 9/11 family members, town officials, and landscape and design professionals. The group was tasked with determining the best presentation for the physical memorial. I didn't hesitate to answer yes. I was ready.

For two years, we met monthly to review and deliberate on

idea submissions for the memorial. We had to sort out the location, design, how it might be used by the public, and numerous other details.

Ultimately, *The Rising*—a memorial by architect Frederick Schwartz—won by unanimous vote. Named after the Bruce Springsteen song, it was placed in Kensico Dam Park in Valhalla, New York, against the backdrop of the Kensico Dam. The eighty-foot structure features 123 intertwined strands—one for each Westchester victim. It is a spectacular and fitting tribute to those 123 lost Westchester citizens, including Mark.

My volunteer work didn't stop there. The synagogue and Rabbi Krantz had treated my family well and made us feel welcome, so we joined. To my relief, I found that I fit in. It worked to my advantage that usually one half of a couple joins a committee. It was rare for both partners to volunteer for the same initiative, so I never stuck out as being single or a widow. I could just do my thing and contribute. Soon enough, I became a synagogue board member and a committee chair.

Meanwhile, therapy got Rachael and me through a certain period in our lives, but those sessions drew to a natural close. Everything seemed fine until I started to sense something else might be percolating. Although I handled plenty of carpooling to and from school, synagogue, and extracurricular activities, Rachael and William seemed to trust only me to make pickups. They refused to be taken home by anyone else, including parents of close friends.

I felt I had to explore this insecurity and nip it in the bud. I also thought my family might be missing something in our healing process: a peer group who understood firsthand what each of us had been going through. There were few single-parent families in town and even fewer widows. Divorce typically meant that the family would split up and scatter to different places.

William was now old enough to understand what had happened

on 9/11, and there was no way I could leave him out of a healing experience. That year, at a preschool holiday concert with most parents in attendance, his grief became obvious. His teachers found me in the auditorium before the performance to inform me of what was happening. I raced over to him.

"Everyone's dad is here," he tearfully said.

I spent several minutes consoling William before sending him off to sing about the joys of Thanksgiving with his classmates. I tried to maintain my composure as I watched him perform. All the while, my mind wrestled with trying to figure out how to provide the right support for him.

After conducting some research, I found an organization, "The Den for Grieving Kids," which was on the tail end of offerings that continued to have some 9/11 family participants.

The biweekly program took place on Wednesday evenings in Greenwich, Connecticut, which wasn't far away. Unlike the session I'd attended a few years earlier, this was a wonderful, warm group and a haven for us to express grief. Rachael and William went into their respective rooms, where they did activities—such as making pillows—and talked about their dad with their respective group leaders—mostly trained volunteers—and other kids. I had my own adult peer group as well.

My kids loved it. William would often shout out ahead of time: "We're going to the den!" They looked forward to the pizza, soda, and ice cream, as well as doing the activities and spending time with their new friends, with whom they shared some unique things. During what was referred to as "circle time," we'd all hold hands and one at a time name the people we'd lost. I found it to be cathartic, beneficial, and interesting—especially listening to the details of others who had died, which helped us feel like we were normal and not alone.

I suppose all these therapeutic efforts worked in concert to help me realize that my house was due for some changes. While Mark and I had viewed it as a "starter home," I was now seeing it as a "*forever* home." I suddenly felt up to the emotional (and occasionally physical) challenge of shifting things around in the bedrooms. I was finally able to sort through and pack up Mark's stuff. I saved what I thought would be important for Rachael and William down the road: business suits and a pair of shoes, several pairs of prescription glasses, Giants and Rangers jerseys, sneakers, a dart set, fraternity bric a brac. yearbooks, photo albums, and other memorabilia from his teen summer camp and teen tour years. I donated the rest of his clothes to charity.

As silly as it may seem, I felt I had to demonstrate to the workers who came and went to and from the house—as well as anyone who might be driving by—that there was a man around. Fretting that someone would realize I was a single mom with two kids and see us as vulnerable, I moved Mark's jacket around the house, as well as his shoes and sneakers. I even put chairs out on the lawn in sets of two. I kept his name on our bank checks. The neighborhood was safe and the people I employed trustworthy, but these tactics gave me additional peace of mind.

Oddly, there was almost no pressure on me from friends or family about dating. Inquiries mostly focused on the children ("How are the kids, are they doing okay?") or on financial matters ("Are you able to stay in your house?" or "Do you need help with anything?"). People mainly steered clear of questions regarding my emotional and mental well-being and relationship status. After a couple of years, however, my perception of being alone shifted. I could now entertain the thought of someone other than Mark being in my life without getting physically ill or anxious. Internet dating was gaining momentum, and I thought this might be a good way to "see what's out there." To avoid being the subject of any rumors and gossip, I didn't accept blind dates or date anyone nearby. I preferred the anonymity of going out with men outside of the area who wouldn't know I was a 9/11 widow. At the time, I just didn't want that to end up being the subject of conversation for an entire evening.

I had an improbable connection with Dan, a forty-year-old Canadian bachelor who now made New York City his home. He was a smart, kind, and soft-spoken man who checked all the right boxes, especially in terms of being "safe" and good with the kids. The relationship lasted for about six months before I ended it. The problem for me was simple lack of chemistry. My daughter summed up what I had been thinking but couldn't admit: "Mom, you can do better."

Jill thought I'd make a mistake and was thinking practically. "You found a nice guy, and he's good to your kids. I'm not sure what more you can hope to expect at this point."

I was willing to take my chances—and why shouldn't I have been choosy? I didn't need a partner just for the sake of having one, and I was comfortable with my life. I didn't see my career vision yet, but I somehow knew it was out there and would come to me in time.

I can be both a mother and a father to my kids. I have a loving, caring, and supportive community of family, friends, and neighbors. I miss Mark and he will always be in our thoughts and hearts. But we are not broken. We are not damaged. We have survived the most tragic of historic events and come out the other side strong. We are finding joy and happiness wherever and however we can. We may not be perfect, but what family is? All I know is that we are going to be okay—and that is what Mark would have wanted most of all.

Epilogue

The Heart Returned

Wall Street, New York City
1 Police Plaza
August 2004

. . . I opened my eyes and exhaled.

Officer Henley removed an object from the metallic box, which I noticed had a numbered identification tag on it. He placed it on the table and remained silent as I studied it.

A gold wedding ring.

Not just any wedding ring, Mark's wedding band. I would recognize it anywhere, although it was no longer round, having been bent into an imperfect oval shape with a sharp indent downward directly into its center. The two telltale signs were the hammered edges and lack of inscription.

The sight took my breath away. I was incapable of speech.

William caught sight of it and exclaimed what I had been thinking but could not express: "Mom! It's a heart!"

I didn't know what protocols might have been in place, but I didn't hesitate another second to pick the ring off the table and examine it closer. For my own edification, I reached into my purse and extracted my own wedding band. I held the two together, side by side. There was no question about it. Aside from the misshapen form of the one the officer had removed from the box, the two were 100 percent identical.

"Wow," I praised the officer. "I can't believe you were right. It's definitely Mark's ring, a perfect match."

Officer Henley smiled knowingly and said simply, "I told you I had it."

I felt like this came at just the right time for me, as I had begun to feel increasingly disconnected from Mark. This heart-shaped ring brought him right back to me.

I had to know more details about its discovery. "How was it found?" I asked.

"Based on the notes I read, it was found very soon after 9/11—likely within the first week," he informed me.

Tears filled my eyes as I repeated in astonishment, "The first week!"

"A first responder saw it in plain sight amidst the rubble and picked it up," he informed me. "Your husband's ring was added to the thousands of other items collected from the site. These past few years, we've gone through the painstaking work of matching everything that was found there to the items that were reported missing."

I couldn't believe my good fortune that no one had made a claim for anything even closely resembling this particular ring. Not only that—it seemed miraculous no one else had mistakenly identified it, perhaps in desperation to possess something that might have belonged to their loved one. This small piece of gold I now held in my hand was destined for me only.

I held the wedding band up to William, who was entranced by it. I wanted to make this moment as special as possible for him. "William, this is your dad's ring."

He seemed as awestruck and excited as I did. "Can I be the one to tell Rachael?" he asked, his light brown eyes widening.

"Sure," I answered, hugging him.

I thanked Officer Henley and shook his hand before William and I departed the police station with the ring. All I could think about on the subway ride was how wonderful it was going to be for us to share this news with our family members.

On the train ride home, I could hardly contain my composure as I became emotionally overwhelmed. The feelings of emptiness and doubt that had become familiar companions took their leave. In their place, a sense of wholeness and contentment. I felt renewed and hopeful.

Mark and I are reconnected. There is no doubt this is a sign. Loved ones are never really gone. We just have to learn to relate to them in a new and different way. I will never again doubt the existence of our connection or of your eternal and enduring love.

I am my Beloved's and my Beloved is mine: Song of Solomon 6:3.

 ## Two More Gifts

Prior to 9/11, I never considered myself a particularly religious or spiritual person. Since then, given everything my family's experienced, I have had a hard time believing there aren't greater forces at work in our world. There are simply too many indicators to ignore or to chalk up to mere coincidence. In addition to the discovery of Mark's heart-shaped ring, two other unusual things occurred at meaningful points in time that signaled Mark's presence in some way.

The first took place after I attended the tenth anniversary 9/11 memorial event at Ground Zero. Notable local and national politicians and public figures were present, including former Secretary of State Hillary Clinton and New York Mayor Michael R. Bloomberg. It was a gorgeous September day, not unlike that fateful Tuesday a decade earlier.

When our family arrived home after the service, I noticed something different than when I left that morning. On the balcony, visible through the sliding glass doors from the kitchen, stood a white dove directly facing us. The bird didn't budge, even when we moved in for a closer look. After several hours of seeing the bird outside, I decided to leave some food and water out for it. The dove ate and drank and eventually felt comfortable enough in my presence to allow me to snap a few photos. Over the next few days, it made our balcony its temporary home. One morning, the bird was gone—and hasn't returned since.

We never had a bird of any kind visit our property for any noticeable length of time before. Of all the types of birds to have shown up at that moment on September 11, why a *white dove*? It struck me as far too biblical to have just been a coincidence. In Judaism, the dove is associated with a sign of life: as a symbol of the human soul, among other things. I'd like to think our visitor was offering comfort to us and perhaps even an acknowledgment on a more spiritual plane.

In 2019, just before the pandemic, my women's study group was to start reading a new book, *Toward a Meaningful Life*, by Menahem Mendel Schneerson and Simon Jacobson. The book is a spiritual road map based on the teachings and wisdom of visionary Rebbe Schneerson, who had been head of the Lubavitcher movement for forty-four years.

"I know that book. I already have a copy," I said to Miriam, our group leader and teacher. "You gave it to me."

She shook her head. "No . . . I don't think I did."

"Are you certain?" I asked, wondering whether I had been thinking of a different book, as she has gifted me with several over the years.

When I returned home, I scavenged the bookshelves for the title. I found the hardcover book on the shelf but was puzzled as to how it arrived there. Tucked inside the pages was a pamphlet, listing various classes and offerings of an unfamiliar religious organization. Intrigued, I shared it with Miriam at the next class.

"Oh yes, I know them. They were a Jewish group based in Brooklyn. They disbanded some time ago."

I continued to try and figure out how I'd obtained the book, especially since it was clear that Miriam hadn't been the one to give it to me. The only explanation was that at some point Mark had been approached in Manhattan by members of this organization. He identified himself as Jewish and was invited to participate in ritual prayer with them. I recalled Mark mentioning to me that he had interacted with such observant men on at least one occasion. I presumed he was gifted this book after having made a financial donation or simply as a token of good will.

The book had sat untouched on the shelf for years. I somehow knew it was there but hadn't considered picking it up until that moment.

Later that day, I dove into reading the book and was struck by how its tone and content closely aligned with the values Mark had embodied. Its profound wisdom on matters such as work, relationships, and education—as well as mental and physical health—were dispensed in a practical and attainable way. I wondered whether Mark would have thought I was measuring up to these markers.

In the years since Mark's passing, I would at times find myself thinking, *What advice would Mark give me? What would he want me to do in this situation?*

One quote from Rebbe Schneersohn has since stuck with me: *"We must translate pain into action and tears into growth."*

I have since vowed to follow those words as a guidepost for the rest of my life.

POSTSCRIPT

As time passes and wounds heal, it's inevitable that some friends and acquaintances will venture off in their own directions. It is with some regret that I haven't remained in close contact with many of the individuals mentioned in this book. For this reason and out of respect for everyone's privacy, I have kept my postscript updates brief and primarily limited to immediate family members.

Rachael Brisman: My daughter received her undergraduate degree from the University of Wisconsin, Madison and a master's degree from Columbia University. Rachael is currently a researcher and pediatric speech pathologist in New York City. Recently, she announced her engagement to her college sweetheart, Eli Silverman, who will graduate from New York University School of Law in 2023.

William Brisman: My son, now a grown man, is following in his father's footsteps to become an attorney. In Fall 2022, he will be attending New York University's School of Law. Ironically, the child who was indifferent to athletics became a State Champion in Track and Field and earned an athletic scholarship to the University of Connecticut, where he graduated with dual degrees in political science and history, as well as English. He doesn't refer to me as "Mom" but as "Coach."

Michelle Brisman Gladstein, PhD: Dr. Brisman, Mark's twin sister, is a neuropsychologist in private practice in Connecticut. She gave birth to a son nine months after 9/11 and named him Mark.

He is presently a college undergraduate and has a younger brother in high school.

Steven Brisman, DMD: Dr. Brisman, Mark's older brother, continues to practice dentistry in Westchester, New York. He dubbed his on-site lab "On the Mark" in honor of his late brother. Steven and his wife, Barbara, are parents of two young adult children.

Jaci Iskols: Mark's older sister, remains married to Rob, her college sweetheart. They have three adult children. Jaci has worked in various administrative capacities over the years and resides in New Jersey.

Jill Katz: My sister remains married to her husband, David. Jill, a stay-at-home mother of four, returned to school to complete a nursing degree and was valedictorian of her program. She lives in suburban Boston.

Roberta Brisman: Roberta, Mark's mom, passed away in December 2002 at sixty-nine years of age after a long battle against cancer.

Jerry Brisman: Jerry, Mark's father, passed away in May 2020 of Parkinson's disease at age eighty-seven.

Eva Brisman: Eva, Jerry's widow, is retired and divides her time between Pennsylvania and Florida. She enjoys golf and playing cards and adores her nine grandchildren.

Martin (Marty) Steuer: My father, affectionately known as Poppy, passed away in January 2021 at age eighty of Parkinson's disease. At the time of his death, my parents were married for fifty-three years.

June Steuer: My mom is retired. She enjoys spending her time with her six devoted grandchildren, gardening, and birdwatching.

Allan Fudim: Mark's mentor and a respected trial attorney passed away in 2007 in Florida at sixty-two years of age.

PHOTOGRAPHS

Mark's photo i.d. circa 1986, around the time we first met. I kept this photo in my wallet for many years.

To this day, I can't believe Mark saved this tiny scrap of paper—the back of a business card—on which I scribbled my phone number when we met at the club.

This is the first photo of Mark and me together, taken in a photo booth on the day we met in the summer of '86. Neither of us had any clue where this mini golf date would ultimately lead.

This is a photo of me taken on the pay phone at my dorm at Hofstra University. I'd like to say I was on one of my many long-distance calls with Mark, but I was probably just posing.

Mark and his family, circa June 1989. From left to right: Michelle, Roberta, Mark (middle bottom), Steven, and Jaci.

My sister, Jill, and me, around 1989.

Mark and I posed for this picture after his graduation from New York University, School of Law. The event took place at Lincoln Center in May 1992.

November 6, 1993: Our wedding day! Mark slides the wedding ring on my finger.

My parents, June and Marty, at our wedding.

Mark and I before attending my ten-year reunion from East Meadow High School on Long Island, circa June 1996. My baby bump is already pretty visible.

Photograph of Mark with newborn baby Rachael in December 1996.

Mark, Rachael, newborn William, and me posing for our first full family photo in August 1999.

One of the few photos I have of Mark in his work attire as he stands in front of the courthouse in the Bronx, NY. I love how poised and "in his element" he looks, although it was only the beginning of his legal career.

Mark—aka "Gym Daddy"—playing with the kids in our house in Armonk, NY, in December 2000.

The Brisman family vacationing together in Florida in February 2001.

Summer 2000: One-year-old William with Mark at the annual Fol-De-Rol Festival in Armonk, NY.

Adventureland, Farmingdale, NY, Labor Day weekend 2001: Mark holds out his cap while on one of the rides with Rachael. Mark seamlessly switched gears from proper professional during the week to one of joyful abandon on the weekends and holidays. He loved spending time with the kids and acting like a child himself.

A photo of "The Rising," a 9/11 memorial in Westchester, NY. I served on the committee that helped bring this work of art to life. Photo credit: John Vecchiolla

Mark's law firm, Harris, Beach & Wilcox, sent this plaque to the families of those employees who were lost on 9/11.

Photographs *197*

While most of the debris from the Twin Towers was deposited in the Fresh Kills Landfill in Staten Island, many 9/11 families were sent small steel fragments of the wreckage as something of a memorial to honor their loved ones. This is a photo of the one I received. Written on the card: "To honor those who were lost on September 11th, 2001, artist Bryan Hunt created the enclosed memorial of recovered steel from the World Trade Center 2003."

Photograph of Eva, Rachael, and Jerry together on a Caribbean cruise, circa 2004.

Portrait of Rachael (9), William (6), and me, circa August 2006.

This dove appeared on the tenth anniversary of 9/11, as soon as we got home from the commemorative ceremony in the city. He stayed for three days. That was his only appearance.

ABOUT THE AUTHOR
Juliette Brisman, MA, LMFT

After the events detailed in *A Heart Returned*, Juliette continued to volunteer in her community and focus primarily on raising her children. She always remembered the impact other professionals and volunteers had on her and her family. Inspired, she trained to become a bereavement facilitator at the Den for Grieving Kids, the same program that had served as a valuable resource for her family. After several years of service, Juliette went on to pursue a career as a mental health professional. She enrolled in the Marriage and Family Therapy program at Fairfield University, receiving her master's degree in 2018 and attaining professional licensure in 2019. Currently, Juliette is a Licensed Marriage and Family Therapist (LMFT) in private practice in Connecticut. She accompanies her clients on their unique journeys through loss and brings empathy and understanding to every client relationship. Juliette is motivated by her ability to empower her clients to move toward growth, healing, and hope. She knows Mark would be proud.

www.ingramcontent.com/pod-product-compliance
Lightning Source LLC
Chambersburg PA
CBHW030331010526
44119CB00036B/457/J